D1225716

前　言

　　我们在去年出版的《走进中国百姓生活——中高级汉语视听说教程》的前言中曾说："我们都是在美国多年从事中文教学的教师，深感目前能使学生通过真实鲜活的汉语了解中国现实社会的视听材料十分匮缺。为此我们编了这部教材。"《走进中国百姓生活》是中高级视听说教材，出于同样的目的，我们现在又编写了《中国百姓身边的故事》这套初中级视听说教材。我们一直在寻找篇幅短小、语言简易的现代中国电视剧，《咱老百姓》是先找到的，《身边的故事》是后找到的，所以根据这两个电视剧编写的教材《走进中国百姓生活》和《中国百姓身边的故事》也是程度高的先问世，程度低的后出版。这两套教材实际上是姊妹篇。据说中国一年在电视上播出上万集电视剧，但都是几十集乃至上百集的连续剧，电视短剧微乎其微。我们在《走进中国百姓生活》的前言中说："中国的电视剧很多，但是短剧可谓凤毛麟角。"到目前为止，我们只发现了《咱老百姓》和《身边的故事》两部短小的系列短剧。根据前者编写的《走进中国百姓生活》适合中文程度较高的学生，出版以来，受到广大师生的欢迎，而且已被韩国出版社引进。

　　《身边的故事》是北京电视台正在播放的电视短剧，每集5分钟，已播放了300多集。这部系列短剧把中国人身边正在发生的故事呈现在我们眼前。我们从中选了20个。这20个短剧反映了北京普通人生活的方方面面。剧中的人物有白领，有外地到北京的打工者，也有摊贩，还有外国旅游者；有老人，有孩子，还有盲人。剧中的人物多种多样，他们的生活色彩缤纷，他们的故事生动有趣。

　　《身边的故事》的语言也以日常口语为主，语言鲜活、生动。每集只有5分钟，无论作为辅助教材还是主教材，都会比较好用。

　　本教材每课包括课文、生词、练习几部分，练习突出了听说。

　　本教材的对象定位于中文程度为初级和中级的学习者。教师可以根据学生的程度和教学需要灵活安排进度。

　　美国戴维斯大学的储诚志教授用"中文助教"软件为我们挑选生词，使我们节省了很多时间。世界图书出版公司在本书出版过程中给与我们很多帮助，在此一并表示感谢。

刘月华　李金玉　刘宪民　葛良彦

PREFACE

In the preface to our *Reality Chinese: A Multi-skill Chinese Course for Intermediate and Advanced Students* published in 2006, we made this statement: "Having taught Chinese in the United States for many years, we were fully aware of the deficiency of the audio-video teaching materials that could help acquaint the students to the contemporary Chinese society through authentic and living language. Precisely because of that, we have compiled this textbook." Still for the same reason, we are now offering this volume of *Scenario Chinese: A Multi-skill Chinese Course for Beginning and Intermediate Students*. These two volumes form a series, even though we have not followed the usual order of publishing the lower-level textbook before the upper-level one.

Thousands of TV series are aired in China every year, but the vast majority of them are lengthy dramas with dozens of episodes. TV series of independent mini-plays are rare. So far we have only discovered two such series, *Folks Like You and Me* 咱老百姓 and *Stories Amid Ourselves* 身边的故事. The upper-level volume of our series consists of plays selected from *Folks Like You and Me*. Since its publication in 2006, it has been well received by teachers and students. Recently, it has been introduced into the Republic of Korea by a Korean press.

Stories Amid Ourselves is a series of mini-plays shown on Beijing Television. Over three hundred plays have been presented, from which we have selected twenty for this present volume. These twenty mini-plays, each lasting about five minutes duration, exhibit different scenarios in the metropolitan life in of Beijing. The characters include white-collar office workers, street peddlers, odd-jobbers from other parts of China, and tourists from foreign countries. Among them some are old and some are young, one is even blind. The plays feature a wide variety of characters whose lives are diverse and colorful and whose stories are vivacious and intriguing.

The plays collected here present vivid and up-to-date spoken Chinese. Since each mini-play conveniently functions as a unit, this volume can be used either as a principal or a supplementary textbook. Each unit includes the text, vocabulary, grammar notes, and exercises, which lay particular emphasis on listening and speaking. The book targets the beginning and intermediate students, and the instructors are encouraged to make adjustments of the pace according to the students' proficiency levels.

We are thankful to Professor Chu Chengzhi of University of California at Davis, who kindly helped us select vocabulary with his computer program "Chinese TA". Thanks are also due editors at the World Publishing Corporation (世界图书出版公司), whose assistance has been crucial in bringing this volume to print.

Liu Yuehua, Li Jinyu, Liu Xianmin, Ge Liangyan

《身边的故事》主题歌

The Theme Song of *Stories Amid Ourselves*

略　语　表

List of Abbreviations

adj.	Adjective	形容词
adv.	Adverb	副词
modal.	Modal verb	能愿动词
conj.	Conjunction	连词
interj.	Interjection	叹词
m.	Measure word	量词
n.	Noun	名词
N.	Proper Noun	专有名词
num.	Numerals	数词
ono.	Onomatopoeia	象声词
part.	Particle	助词
pron.	Pronoun	代词
prep.	Preposition	介词
t.	Time word	时间词
v.	Verb	动词
vc.	Verb plus complement	动补结构
vo.	Verb plus object	动宾结构

目 录

第十一课 穿错了

You Dressed Yourself Improperly

编剧：李杨

人物 （Characters）

张大嫂（Zhāng dàsǎo）——四十多岁，看上去比较邋遢。

张大哥（Zhāng dàgē）——四十多岁。

中年妇女（zhōngnián fùnǚ）——四十多岁。

小郑（Xiǎo Zhèng）——男，二十岁，市场管理员。

医生（yīshēng）——三十多岁。

---

1. 大嫂	dàsǎo	n.	older brother's wife (form of address for a married woman about one's own age)
2. 看上去	kàn shangqu		look like
3. 比较	bǐjiào	adv.	rather
4. 邋遢	lāta	adj.	slovenly; sloppy
5. 大哥	dàgē	n.	older brother (form of address for a man about one's own age)
6. 中年	zhōngnián	n.	middle age; middle-aged
7. 妇女	fùnǚ	n.	woman

课 文 Text

张大嫂：哎哟，天哪，都^N1快九点了，你也不叫我一声，一会儿**早市**
该关门了。

张大哥：哎，干吗去？

张大嫂：买菜去啊。

张大哥：你也不穿件衣服。

张大嫂：谁没穿呐，这不是**衣裳**？

张大哥：你这也叫衣服？**浑身蓝白道**，就跟那医院病人似的……

张大嫂：你才**有病**呢，出门儿买个菜^N2，还得穿得**西服革履**的呀？

张大哥：不管怎么说，你穿得也得像点儿样啊^N3？

张大嫂：行了，行了，**少废话**，一会儿该**买不着**活鱼了。

张大哥：哎，哎，我说……

中年妇女：哎，张大嫂，买菜去啊？

张　大　嫂：买菜去。

---

8. 早市	zǎoshì	n.	morning marketplace
9. 衣裳	yīshang	n.	clothes
10. 浑身	húnshēn	n.	from head to toe; all over
11. 道	dào	n.	stripe
12. 有病	yǒu bìng	vo.	be sick; have illness
13. 西服革履	xīfú gélǚ		dressed up (literally: Western suit and leather shoes)
14. 废话	fèihuà	n.	nonsense
15. 买不着	mǎi bu zháo	vc.	unable to buy (something)

中年妇女：嘿，您今天够**潮**的啊[N4]，还真有点儿**审美观点**。

张 大 嫂：真的？

中年妇女：是啊，您瞧您今天穿的这套衣裳，真像电影里那个横路竞二。

张 大 嫂：我说你呀，狗嘴里**吐**不出**象牙**来[N5]！

医　　生：哎，同志，我是附近**青山医院**的医生，今天早上我们一个病人跑出来了，有人看见她跑到你们这里来了，能不能麻烦你帮我们找一下？

小　　郑：你能不能跟我们**描述**一下她的**特征**？

医　　生：是个女的，四十多岁，短**头发**，**身上**穿着**浅蓝色**的带**条纹**的**病号**服，外面还穿着一个**马夹**……

小　　郑：哎，你这样，你给我留个电话，我一有**线索立马通知**你，好不好，你说……

16.	潮	cháo	n. / adj.	fashion; fashionable
17.	审美	shěnměi	v.	appreciate beauty; aesthetics; aesthetical
18.	观点	guāndiǎn	n.	point of view; standpoint
19.	吐	tǔ	v.	spit
20.	象牙	xiàngyá	n.	ivory
21.	青山医院	Qīngshān Yīyuàn	N.	Green Hill Hospital
22.	描述	miáoshù	v.	describe
23.	特征	tèzhēng	n.	characteristic; feature
24.	头发	tóufa	n.	hair (on the head)
25.	身上	shēn shang		on one's body
26.	浅蓝色	qiǎnlánsè	n.	light blue
27.	条纹	tiáowén	n.	stripe
28.	病号	bìnghào	n.	hospitalized patient
29.	马夹	mǎjiá	n.	vest
30.	线索	xiànsuǒ	n.	clue; trace
31.	立马	lìmǎ	adv.	immediately
32.	通知	tōngzhī	v. / n.	notify; inform

鱼　　贩：得了，**大姐**，十三块二。

张大嫂：十三块一毛八，这不上面写着吗？得得得[N6]，算十三块行了吧。

鱼　　贩：成，十三就十三。给，大姐，鱼杀好了。

张大嫂：哎呀，小伙子，坏了，我忘了带钱了。

鱼　　贩：您没带钱你买什么鱼啊？[N7] 您这不是逗吗？你**瞅**，这鱼都杀死了，你说这死鱼谁要啊，是不是？

张大嫂：你别急，你别急，我回去给你拿去行吧。

鱼　　贩：回……回去？回去我哪儿知道你回不回来，你说！

张大嫂：你怎么这么说话啊？

（画外音：是个女的，四十多岁，短头发，身上穿着浅蓝色带条纹的那种的病号服。）

张大嫂：我又不是成心没带钱！

小　　郑：哎，咱别吵，别吵，别吵别吵，大姐，我是市场管理员，有什么问题咱们慢慢儿谈。

张大嫂：是啊，我又不是成心没带钱，谁愿意这样啊。

小　　郑：别别别，别说了，把大姐**扶**到办公室，慢点儿慢点儿。

小　　郑：这钱你甭要了，你知道她是什么人吗？她这儿有病。

鱼　　贩：不会吧，我看她挺**正常**的……

33.	鱼贩	yúfàn	n.	fish seller
34.	大姐	dàjiě	n.	eldest sister (a form of address for a woman about one's own age)
35.	杀	shā	v.	kill
36.	瞅	chǒu	v.	take a look; look at
37.	扶	fú	v.	support with the hand
38.	正常	zhèngcháng	adj.	normal

张大嫂：我跟你说呀，我真的不是不想给他钱。我是早晨着急出门儿，所以没换衣裳就……

小　郑：大姐，大姐，您别着急，来，您坐，您这事儿我**处理不了**，等一会儿我们**领导**来吧。

小　郑：你**盯紧**了，别让病人跑了，我现在就去给医院打电话。

小　郑：喂，青山医院吧？你们的病人找到了。

医　生：找到了，找到了，谢谢你们了。

小　郑：好，那你们赶紧来我们办公室接人吧。

医　生：接人？还接什么人？我们已经把病人接回来了。

小　郑：啊?!

小　郑：哟，大姐，真是**对不住**您。是**这么回事儿**，今天早上从那个青山医院跑出来个病人，我这看您这**身打扮**……

张大嫂：**闹**了半天，你们是把我**当成**了……

张大哥：行，行行行。什么也别说了，咱们赶紧回家。

39. 处理不了	chǔlǐ bù liǎo	vc.	unable to handle (an issue or a matter)
不了	bù liǎo		(complement following a verb indicating not being able to)
40. 领导	lǐngdǎo	n.	leader; superior
41. 盯紧	dīng jǐn	vc.	keep an eye on (somebody) closely; watch
42. 对不住	duì bu zhù	vc.	be sorry; apologize to
43. 这么回事儿	zhème huí shìr		it was like this
44. 身	shēn	m.	set (of clothes)
45. 打扮	dǎban	n./v.	dress, what one wears; dress up, make up
46. 闹	nào	v.	make a fuss
47. 当成	dàng chéng	vc.	take (someone) for (someone else)

张大嫂：你们太**过分**了你们。

小 郑：真不好意思。

张大嫂：太**不像话**了。

张大哥：我看你穿这身打扮就出了门儿，一猜就知道你没带钱……
怎么样，以后还这么打扮出去吗？

张大嫂：行了，你就**饶**了我吧。

张大哥：以后**穿衣戴帽**要**认清**场合，什么样的场合穿什么样的衣服。
你看，在**海边**游泳穿**游泳衣**那很自然，你要是把游泳衣穿
到大**马路**上，那人家还**不定**把你当成什么呢。

张大嫂：看来这以后穿衣服啊，还真得**讲点儿规矩**。我这叫**吃一堑，
长一智**[N8]。

张大哥：是啊。

48. 过分	guòfèn	adj.	excessive
49. 不像话	bú xiàng huà		absurd; outrageous
50. 饶	ráo	v.	forgive; spare
51. 穿衣戴帽	chuān yī dài mào		get dressed (literally: to put on the clothes and the hat)
52. 认清	rèn qīng	vc.	recognize; see clearly
53. 海边	hǎibiān	n.	seashore
54. 游泳衣	yóuyǒngyī	n.	swimming suit
55. 马路	mǎlù	n.	street
56. 不(一)定	bù (yì) dìng		no one knows; possibly
57. 讲(点儿)规矩	jiǎng (diǎnr) guīju	vo.	go by the rules
58. 吃一堑，长一智	chī yí qiàn, zhǎng yí zhì		(see note 8)

注释 Notes

1. "都":

可以表示"已经"的意思。

"都" carries the meaning of "already".

(1) 哎哟，天哪，都快九点了。

Gee, it's almost nine!

(2) 她都懂了，你就别再讲了。

She's got it. No need for you to say it again.

(3) 天都黑了，快回家吧。

It's dark now. Let's go home.

2. "出门买个菜，……":

"出门买个菜"中的"个"不是量词"个"的一般用法，即不表示"菜"的单位、量等，有表示动作比较随便的作用。

Here "个" is not a measure word for the noun that follows. Rather, it is used to downplay the importance of the action or make it sound more casual.

(1) 出门买个菜，还得穿得西服革履的呀？

It is only grocery shopping, and do you want me to get dressed up?

(2) 他太寂寞了，希望常常有人跟他说个话，散散步什么的。

He is too lonely, and hopes to have someone to often chat or take a walk with.

(3) 你呀，真节省，连看个电影都舍不得。

You are really thrifty and don't even go to see movies.

3. "你穿得也得像点儿样啊":

At least you should be dressed decently.

这里的意思是穿衣服应该符合人的身份、经济条件和场合等。比如对经济条件比较好的来说，"穿得像点样儿"就是不能穿得太差。一个人如果上街就不应该穿睡衣，出席正式的宴会不能穿得太随便等等。

The sentence suggests that the way a person is dressed should be consistent with his or her status and economic condition as well as the nature of

the occasion.

4. **"够潮的啊"**：

You are really fashionable.

"潮"的意思是新潮、时髦。

"潮"，which is usually used as a noun，functions here as an adjective. It means "trendy" or "modish".

5. **"狗嘴里吐不出象牙来"**：

俗语。意思是：狗的嘴里吐不出来象的牙齿。比喻坏人说不出好话。

Literally, this popular saying means that ivory never comes out of a dog's mouth. Metaphorically，it suggests that a bad person should never be expected to say anything nice.

6. **"得得得"**：

用来制止别人（继续）说话或做事。

This colloquial formula is sometimes used in trying to stop someone from continuing to say or do something.

（1）张大嫂：十三块一毛八，这不上面写着吗？得得得，算十三块行了吧。

　　Sister Zhang：Thirteen eighteen，isn't it written on it? Fine，fine，fine，
　　　　　　　　　round it to thirteen，OK?

这里"得得得"是用来制止对方多要钱。

Here Sister Zhang uses "得得得" to stop the seller from continuing to argue.

（2）得得得，别说了，就这么定了吧。

OK，OK，OK，no more of it. It's now settled.

（3）得得得，你走吧，别再算了。

Alright，alright，you go your way and stop calculating.

7. **"您没带钱你买什么鱼啊"**：

You didn't bring any money，and you want to buy fish?

这是一个反问句，意思是：你既然没有带钱，就不应该买鱼。

This rhetorical question suggests：Since you have no money on you，you shouldn't be trying to buy any fish.

8. **"吃一堑，长一智"**：

Experience of failure fosters wisdom.

"吃"的意思是"经历""经受""堑"是深沟，"吃一堑"比喻经历一次失败、挫折。"长"的意思是"增长"，"智"是"智慧、聪明、才智"。

这个成语的意思是：经历一次失败、挫折，或犯一次错误，能增长一份见识，能变得更聪明一些。

The verb "吃" here means "to suffer" or "to experience", and "堑" means a deep ditch, which serves as a metaphor for a failure or setback. "长", as a verb here, means "to grow" or "to cultivate", and "智" stands for "智慧" (wisdom) or "才智" (talent and intelligence). More examples：

（1）看来这以后穿衣服啊，还真得讲点儿规矩。我这叫吃一堑，长一智。

　　　It seems I will really have to pay attention to what I wear in the future. This is truly a case of learning from mistakes.

（2）犯错误不要紧，吃一堑，长一智嘛。

　　　It's alright to make mistakes. Don't you say "Experience of failure fosters wisdom"?

（3）你这次上当了应该接受教训，要吃一堑，长一智。

　　　You were deceived. You should learn a lesson and gain something from this mistake.

听说练习　Listening & Speaking Exercises

■ 一、课文理解 Text Comprehension

（一）根据故事情节选择适当的答案

Please choose the most appropriate answer based on the story

1. 今天张大嫂出门（　　）

　　A. 没穿衣裳

　　B. 穿睡觉的衣服（像医院病人穿的）

　　C. 穿得西服革履的

2. 青山医院的一个病人跑到哪儿去了？（　　）

　　A. 电影院　　　　　　B. 菜市场　　　　　　C. 市场管理员办公室那边

3. 鱼贩不高兴是因为张大嫂（　　）

　　A. 穿得奇怪　　　　　B. 话说得太多　　　　　C. 要买鱼却没钱

4. 小郑是（　　）

　　A. 鱼贩　　　　　　　B. 市场管理员　　　　　C. 医生

5. 大家把张大嫂扶到办公室是因为（　　）

　　A. 她年纪大了

　　B. 被鱼贩气坏了

　　C. 以为她是个病人

6. 小郑的领导要来（　　）

　　A. 处理张大嫂　　　B. 送张大嫂回医院　　C. 接张大嫂回家

7. 张大嫂很生气，因为大家把它当成了（　　）

　　A. 病人　　　　　　　B. 鱼贩　　　　　　　C. 小偷

（二）根据课文判断下面句子意思的正误

State whether the following statements are true or false based on the story

1. （　　）张大哥有病了。

2. （　　）今天张大嫂要去医院。

3.（　　）张大哥觉得张大嫂衣裳穿得不好看。

4.（　　）张大嫂没换衣服就去市场了是因为他很相信自己的审美观。

5.（　　）青山医院的一位四十多岁的女病人跑了。

6.（　　）鱼贩很不高兴是因为他把张大嫂要买的鱼都杀死了，但张大嫂说没带钱。

7.（　　）小郑以为张大嫂是青山医院跑出来的那个病人。

8.（　　）小郑给青山医院打电话时，那个病人还没找到呢。

（三）先听故事叙述，然后复述故事

Listen to the narrative first and then retell the story

　　张大嫂要去早市买菜，她怕去晚了买不着活鱼了，所以忙得没换衣服，穿着睡衣就去了。张大哥要他换换衣服再去，她反而说张大哥废话多。

　　这天早上，附近青山医院的一个病人跑了，有人看见她跑到菜市场去了。

　　医院给市场管理办公室打电话，请求他们帮助。他们还告诉市场管理员小郑这个病人是位四十多岁的女人，短头发，身上穿着浅蓝色的带条纹的病号服，外面还穿一个马夹。

　　小郑一到菜市场就看见正在跟鱼贩争吵的张大嫂。张大嫂的打扮、年龄等让小郑以为她就是医院要找的病人。小郑叫人把张大嫂扶到办公室后立刻给青山医院打电话，但是医院的人告诉他病人已经找到了。这时张大嫂才明白原来他们把她当成病人了。

　　这件事让张大嫂认识到以后穿衣戴帽还真得讲点儿规矩，不然会闹出笑话来。

■ 二、词语使用 Application of Vocabulary and Grammar

（一）选择题

Choose the item that is grammatically correct

1. 哎哟，天哪，_____快九点了。你也不叫我一声，一会儿早市该关门了。

　　A. 很　　　　　　　　B. 就　　　　　　　　C. 都

2. 你这也叫衣服？浑身蓝白道，就跟医院病人_____。

　　A. 似的　　　　　　　B. 很像　　　　　　　C. 的样子

3. 你_____有病呢，出门买个菜，还得穿得西服革履的呀？

    A. 刚   B. 就   C. 才

4. _____怎么说，你穿得也得像点儿样啊？

    A. 就是   B. 不管   C. 虽然

5. 你能不能跟我们描述_____她的特征？

    A. 很多   B. 一下   C. 很好

6. 十三块一毛八，这不上面写着吗？得得得，_____十三块行了吧。

    A. 算   B. 是   C. 有

（二）选择题

Circle the answer that best reflects the meaning of the underlined portion of the sentence

1. 不管怎么说，你穿得也得<u>像点儿样</u>啊？（   ）

    A. 像别人一样

    B. 不能太随便

    C. 有一点儿像

    D. 样子很像

2. 您没带钱你买什么鱼啊？您这不是<u>逗</u>吗？（   ）

    A. 有意思

    B. 不可能

    C. 有兴趣

    D. 开玩笑

3. 十三块一毛八，这不上面写着吗？<u>得得得</u>，算十三块行了吧。（   ）

    A. 看看看

    B. 来来来

    C. 好了，好了

    D. 决定了

4. 哎，你这样，你给我留个电话，我一有线索<u>立马</u>通知你，好不好？

                                     （   ）

    A. 骑马

    B. 站马

    C. 赶快

    D. 马上

5. 我说你呀，<u>狗嘴里吐不出象牙来</u>！（　　）
   A. 你跟狗一样
   B. 说不出好话来
   C. 有象牙但吐不出来
   D. 狗嘴里没有象牙

6. 嘿，您今天够<u>潮</u>的啊，还真有点儿审美观点。（　　）
   A. 时髦
   B. 好看
   C. 不干
   D. 有水

（三）选择适当的词语，替换句中的画线部分
Choose the most appropriate words to replace the underlined parts

A. 都	B. 得得得	C. 成心的	D. 够潮的
E. 吃一堑，长一智		F. 狗嘴里吐不出象牙	

1. 天<u>已经</u>黑了，快回家吧。
2. <u>行了，行了</u>，少废话，一会儿该买不着活鱼了。
3. 犯错误不要紧，<u>有了一次教训，下次就不会再错了</u>。
4. 嘿，张大嫂，您今天穿的真够<u>时髦</u>的啊！
5. 我说你呀，<u>坏人说不出好话来</u>！
6. 我又不是<u>故意</u>没带钱，谁愿意这样啊。

（四）用所给词语完成对话
Complete the following dialogues with the items provided in the parenthesis

1. （赶紧，太不像话了，闹了半天，对不住）
   小　郑：大姐，真是＿＿＿＿＿您。我这看您这身打扮以为您是从青
   　　　　山医院跑出来的那个病人。
   张大嫂：＿＿＿＿＿，你们是把我当成了……
   张大哥：行了。什么也别说了，咱们＿＿＿＿＿回家吧。
   张大嫂：你们也＿＿＿＿＿！

2. （太过分了，成心）
   鱼　贩：你看，你要的鱼我都杀死了，你说这死鱼我卖给谁呀？您这
   　　　　不是＿＿＿＿＿给我找麻烦吗?!
   张大嫂：你别急，鱼我拿走，我回家给你拿钱去。
   鱼　贩：鱼放在这儿，不能拿走，你还想骗我?

张大嫂：你怎么这么说话啊？＿＿＿＿＿＿！

3.（怎么样；得得得；看来；吃一堑，长一智）

张大哥：你出去以前我就叫你换换衣服，你不听。＿＿＿＿＿＿，以后还这么打扮出去吗？

张大嫂：＿＿＿＿＿＿，你就饶了我吧。＿＿＿＿＿＿这以后穿衣服啊，还真得讲点儿规矩。我这叫＿＿＿＿＿＿。

（五）角色扮演 Role play

Make a dialogue with a classmate. One party plays Zhang dasao, and the other plays Zhang dage. The conversation takes place at their home after the incident at the market. Your dialogue should incorporate the provided items.

张大嫂	张大哥
After enduring the incident, you feel dispirited and angry. You failed to buy the fish which was the reason you hurried to the market in the first place. It took hours before you finally realized that you had been taken for a run away mental patient because of the clothes you were wearing. How outrageously ridiculous they were! You beg your husband for pardon when he tells you off for not listening to his advice. The incident has taught you the importance of dressing properly. You think you are now smarter because of it.	You want your wife to know that her failure to take your advice has resulted in this unfortunate incident. You recount how she reacted at your suggestions in the morning before she went to the market. You stress that one must dress in accordance with the occasion. Would one wear a swimming suit in the street?
1. 鱼也没买成　　2. 太不像话 3. 闹了半天　　4. 把我当成 5. 饶了我　　　6. 讲点儿规矩 7. 吃一堑，长一智	1. 这身打扮　　2. 一猜就 3. 有病　　　4. 少废话 5. 西服革履　　6. 穿衣戴帽 7. 场合　　　8. 游泳衣 9. 大马路上

■ 三、课堂讨论 Discussion

1. 张大嫂为什么被误认为是一个从医院跑出来的病人？

2. 有人说"在什么场合穿什么衣服是很有讲究的"，你同意吗？为什么？

3. "穿什么衣服是自己的选择，是一个人的自由"，对这种说法你有什么看法？

第十二课 姐 姐

Sister

编剧：沈汀

（根据陈镝提供的故事改编）

人物 (Characters)

秦悦（Qín Yuè）——女，高三学生。

方凯（Fāng Kǎi）——男，初三学生。

课 文 Text

秦 悦：我可以进来吗？

秦 悦：你不说话就是默认啦。

秦 悦：我可以跟你认识一下吗？

秦 悦：啊，我叫秦悦，理工大学附中高三年级学生，团支部宣传

1. 高三	gāo sān		High school senior
2. 初三	chū sān		Middle school 3rd-year
3. 默认	mòrèn	v.	give tacit consent to; tacitly approve
4. 理工大学 附中	Lǐgōng Dàxué Fùzhōng	N.	High school affiliated to University of Science and Technology
5. 团支部	tuánzhībù	n.	Branch of Youth League

委员，英语课代表。我是双鱼座，O型血。

方　凯：方凯。

秦　悦：还有呢？

方　凯：初三。

秦　悦：今天天气真好，阳光明媚。哎，晒太阳有利于[N1]钙的吸收，你不想出去转转吗？

方　凯：我不想去。

秦　悦：嗨！

方　凯：嗨！

秦　悦：怎么出来啦？

方　凯：刚做完检查……

秦　悦：坐啊。

秦　悦：能告诉我，你得的是什么病吗？

方　凯：反正比你（的）病厉害。

6.	宣传委员	xuānchuán wěiyuán	n.	committee member in charge of communication and public relations
7.	英语课代表	yīngyǔ kè dàibiǎo		monitor for English class
8.	双鱼座	shuāngyúzuò	n.	Pisces
9.	O型血	Ou xíng xuè		O Type blood
10.	阳光明媚	yángguāng míngmèi		beautiful sunshine
11.	晒太阳	shài tàiyáng	vo.	sun-bathe
12.	有利于	yǒulìyú		be beneficial
13.	钙	gài	n.	calcium
14.	吸收	xīshōu	v.	absorption
15.	转	zhuàn	v.	stroll around

秦　悦：嗨，你真逗，比什么有比得病的呀？你到底^{N2}是什么病啊？

方　凯：**癌症**……

秦　悦：想哭你就哭吧，哭完了，心里也许能**轻松**点儿。其实**想开**了，也没有什么大不了的^{N3}，现在**医学发展**这么快，癌症不一定就**等于死亡**。天不是还没塌下来吗？^{N4}**地球**不是还在转吗？^{N5}春天不是说来就来了吗？^{N6}

方　凯：我可没**心情**听你作**诗**。

秦　悦：可春天本来就是一首诗**摆**在你**面前**，就别跟自己**过意不去**^{N7}啦，**与其痛不欲生**，不如^{N8}**争分夺秒**、**快快乐乐**地过好每一天。

16.	得病	dé bìng	vo.	suffer from (disease); become ill
17.	到底	dàodǐ	adv.	after all
18.	癌症	áizhèng	n.	cancer
19.	轻松	qīngsōng	adj.	relaxed
20.	想开	xiǎng kāi	vc.	take things easy; be resigned to misfortune
21.	医学	yīxué	n.	medical science; medicine
22.	发展	fāzhǎn	v.	develop; advance
23.	等于	děngyú	v.	equal to; equivalent to
24.	死亡	sǐwáng	v.	death
25.	塌	tā	v.	fall down
26.	地球	dìqiú	n.	earth
27.	心情	xīnqíng	n.	mood
28.	诗	shī	n.	poetry; verse
29.	摆	bǎi	v.	put; place
30.	面前	miàn qián		in front of
31.	过意不去	guòyì bu qù		(see note 7)
32.	与其	yǔqí	conj.	rather than; better than
33.	痛不欲生	tòng bú yù shēng		be overwhelmed with sorrow or grieve to the extent of wishing to die
34.	争分夺秒	zhēng fēn duó miǎo		seize every minute
35.	快快乐乐	kuài kuài lè lè		happily

方　凯：我可快乐不起来。

秦　悦：嗨，其实呀，快乐的方式有很多种。**古人说，学而时习之不亦说乎**，其实我们的**祖先**很早就把学习当成一种**乐趣**啦。这样吧，从明天起咱俩一起复习功课好吗？我也好^{N9}有个**伴**儿，你准备**中考**，我准备**高考**，行吗？

方　凯：我不想参加中考了。

秦　悦：你不参加中考干吗去？你不仅要**迎接**考试，还要迎接**命运**的考验。我相信，你一定能行的。来，**男子汉**可要说话算话。

方　凯：嗯！

秦　悦：如果没猜错的话，这个……是你的？

方　凯：是我的，我以为再也**用不着了**……

36.	古人	gǔrén	n. ancients; forefathers
37.	学而时习之不亦说乎	xué ér shí xí zhī bú yì yuè hū	"Is it not pleasant to learn with a constant perseverance and application?"
38.	祖先	zǔxiān	n. ancestry; ancestors
39.	乐趣	lèqù	n. joy; pleasure
40.	伴儿	bànr	n. companion
41.	中考	zhōngkǎo	n. high school entrance examination
42.	高考	gāokǎo	n. college or university entrance examination
43.	迎接	yíngjiē	v. welcome; meet
44.	命运	mìngyùn	n. destiny; fate
45.	男子汉	nánzǐhàn	n. a real man; true man
46.	用不着	yòng bu zháo	vc. not necessary; useless

秦　悦：还要我第二次再帮你捡回来吗？

秦　悦：叫我一声姐姐！

秦　悦：你不想知道我得的是什么病吗？

方　凯：什么病？

秦　悦：和你一样，不过，我是血癌，也就是，白血病。

（画外音：秦悦！你好吗？我的病情已稳定了。出院那天，本想和你去告别，可你正在化疗，我就悄悄走了。你的病比我严重，但我一点儿都没看出来，不是我笨，而是你非常勇敢……有一件事，现在想起来还在后悔，我居然[N10]没叫你一声姐姐。如果没有你这个姐姐，也许我永远也不会坐在这明亮的教室里。别忘了咱们的约定，今年我中考，明年你高考，答应我，姐姐……）

47.	捡回来	jiǎn huílai	vc.	pick up
48.	血癌	xuè'ái	n.	leukemia
49.	白血病	báixuèbìng	n.	leukemia
50.	病情	bìngqíng	n.	state of an illness; patient's condition
51.	稳定	wěndìng	adj.	stable; steady
52.	出院	chū yuàn	vo.	be discharged from hospital
53.	告别	gàobié	v.	bid farewell to; say goodbye to
54.	化疗	huàliáo	n./v.	chemotherapy
55.	悄悄	qiāo qiāo	adv.	quietly
56.	看出来	kàn chulai	vc.	make out; see
57.	笨	bèn	adj.	stupid; foolish
58.	而是	érshì	conj.	but (rather)
59.	勇敢	yǒnggǎn	adj.	brave; courageous
60.	后悔	hòuhuǐ	v.	regret
61.	居然	jūrán	adv.	unexpectedly; to one's surprise
62.	永远	yǒngyuǎn	adv.	always; forever
63.	明亮	míngliàng	adj.	well-lit; bright
64.	约定	yuēdìng	v.	promise
65.	答应	dāying	v.	answer; respond

注释 Notes

1. **"于"**：

　　"于"用在动词或形容词后，可以表示介词"对"的意思。多用于书面语。

　　"于" is a preposition meaning "to，for". It is mostly a formal term.

（1）哎，晒太阳有利于钙的吸收，你不想出去转转吗？

　　Hey，sunshine is good for absorption of calcium. Don't you want to go and take a stroll outside?

（2）听录音不仅有助于提高听力，而且对提高口语也有好处。

　　Listening to recording not only helps your listening comprehension，but also is good for improving your oral proficiency.

（3）他已经习惯于北方的生活了。

　　He's already accustomed to life in the North.

2. **"到底"**：

　　"到底"在这里用于追问。

　　"到底"（"after all"）here is used to prod someone for an answer.

（1）嗨，你真逗，比什么有比得病的呀？你到底是什么病啊？

　　You are so funny. You can compare anything but diseases. There's no such thing as "my disease is better than yours". What disease do you have anyways?

（2）你刚才说去，现在又说不去，你到底去不去呀？

　　You said a moment ago that you wouldn't go，and you are now saying that you will. Are you going or not?

（3）老师好像说我们明天有考试，可是小李说没有。明天到底有没有考试啊？

　　The teacher said there would be a test tomorrow，but Little Li said there would be none. Is there indeed a test tomorrow or not?

3. **"没有什么大不了的"**：

　　It's nothing serious.

　　"没有什么大不了"的意思是"（情况、问题）不严重"。口语。

"没有什么大不了", is a colloquial expression, it means "nothing serious or significant".

本剧中"其实想开了，也没有什么大不了的，现在医学发展这么快，癌症并不一定就等于死亡"。意思是：其实想开了你的情况也并不是那么严重，那么可怕。

In this lesson "其实想开了，也没有什么大不了的，……" means "Actually, if you really think about it, it's not that terrible."

4. **"天不是没塌下来吗"**：

这是个反问句，意思是：天没有塌下来，没有到世界末日。比喻情况没有那么严重、可怕。

"The sky hasn't fallen, has it?" This is a rhetorical sentence, meaning "this is not the end of the world".

5. **"地球不是还在转吗"**：

Isn't the earth still turning?

这也是一个反问句，比喻生活还在正常进行。

This is also a rhetorical question, indicating that life is going on as usual.

6. **"春天不是说来就来了吗"**：

Hasn't spring just arrived like this?

"说……就……了"的意思是某动作、事情或变化很快就要发生，或发生得很快。口语。

"说……就……了" is used to indicate that changes take place or have taken place quickly, almost in the blink of an eye.

(1) 你怎么说哭就哭啊？

Why are you crying all of a sudden?

(2) 大雨说下就下，快把窗户关上吧。

The rain is coming just as we're talking about it. Please close the window quickly.

(3) 他这个人说翻脸就翻脸，你跟他说话要多注意一点儿。

He is a person who gets upset really easily. You need to be careful when you talk to him.

7. **"过意不去"**：

"过意不去"本来的意思是：因为自己对别人做了不太应该做的事而心中不安。

"过意不去" means to feel bad or guilty because one did something that hurt other people.

(1) 我昨天回家很晚，没带钥匙，家里又没有门铃，只好大声敲门，结果把邻居都吵醒了，很过意不去。

Yesterday I went home late, and I realized I forgot to bring my keys. My apartment has no doorbell, so I had to knock on the door loudly. I woke up all the neighbors, and I fell really bad.

现在不少人用"过意不去"表示"为难"的意思，如本剧，而这个意思本来应用"过不去"表示。

Nowadays some people use "过意不去" in the sense of "giving someone a hard time", which is originally said as "过不去", such as in this lesson.

(2) 可春天本来就是一首诗摆在你面前，就别再跟自己过意不去啦，与其痛不欲生，不如争分夺秒、快快乐乐地过好每一天。

But spring itself is a poem placed before your eyes. Don't give yourself hard time. It's better to live life to the fullest than to allow yourself to be so overwhelmed by your grief.

这个句子也可改为：可春天本来就是一首诗摆在你面前，就别再跟自己过不去啦。

Therefore, for the sentence above, one can also use "过不去" instead of "过意不去".

8. "与其……，不如……"：

书面语用得较多。

"与其……，不如……" is a rather formal expression.

"与其……，不如……"两个连词后的句子表示两种可供选择的情况，说话人在权衡之后，选择了"不如……"的情况。

"与其" and "不如", as conjunctions, introduce two choices. The speaker, after considering pros and cons, chooses the latter headed by "不如".

(1) 与其痛不欲生，不如争分夺秒、快快乐乐地过好每一天。

You'd rather enjoy every minute of life than to allow yourself to be over-whelmed by your grief.

(2) 天气这么好，与其坐在家里看电视，不如去公园散步。

The weather is so nice. We'd rather take a walk in the park than watch TV at home.

(3) 现在是网络时代，与其买报纸找广告，不如上网看看。

It's the age of the internet, and one would rather surf the net than read ads in the newspaper.

9. **"好"**：

"好"用在第二个分句中，意思是：为了对某事或事情的某个方面有好处或方便。口语。

"好" used in front of a verb, means "in order to, so that, for the convenience/purpose of doing..."

(1) 从明天起咱俩一起复习功课好吗？我也好有个伴儿，你准备中考，我准备高考，行吗？

Starting from tomorrow, can we study together—you prepare for your high school exam, and I prepare for my college exam? This way, I can have a study partner.

(2) 今天晚上早点儿睡觉，明天考试好有精神。

(You) go to bed early tonight, so that tomorrow you will have a lot of energy to take the test.

(3) 你把证件给我，我好替你去取机票。

Give me your ID, so that I can get the plane ticket for you.

"为了"也表示目的，但是通常用在第一个分句中。"为了"在书面语和口语中都可以用。

"为了" is also used to introduce a purpose, but it usually occurs in the first clause, and it fits both the colloquial and formal styles. For example, sentence (2) and (3) above can be changed into the following：

(4) 为了明天考试有精神，你今天晚上早点儿睡觉吧。

(5) 为了替你去取机票，把你的身份证给我吧。

10. **"居然"**：

surprisingly

语气副词"居然"表示出乎意料，说话人认为不应该、不可能或很难发生的事情发生了。

"居然", as an adverbial of modality, suggests that the speaker is surprised at some unexpected event or happening.

(1) 有一件事，现在想起来还在后悔，我居然没有叫你一声姐姐。

One thing that I will always regret whenever I think about it is that I didn't even call you "sister" once.

（2）这次考试他好像根本没复习，居然得了100分。

He didn't even study for this test, and surprisingly, he got 100.

（3）现在是冬天，他居然穿着 T 恤衫上街。

It's winter, and can you believe he goes out wearing a T-shirt!

听说练习　Listening & Speaking Exercises

■ 一、课文理解 Text Comprehension

（一）根据故事情节选择适当的答案

Please choose the most appropriate answer based on the story

1. 秦悦跟方凯以前（　　）

   A. 认识　　　　　　　B. 不认识　　　　　　C. 在学校见过面

2. 方凯不想跟秦悦出去转转，因为他（　　）

   A. 不喜欢秦悦　　　B. 不认识秦悦　　　　C. 为自己的病很难过

3. 方凯认为得了癌症（　　）

   A. 就没有希望了　　B. 地球还会转　　　　C. 没什么大不了的

4. 秦悦认为得了癌症（　　）

   A. 她可以快乐

   B. 她可以作诗

   C. 不一定就会死

5. 秦悦想让方凯跟她一起（　　）

   A. 每天出去转

   B. 复习功课准备考试

   C. 作诗

6. 秦悦帮助了方凯（　　）

   A. 使他中考考得很好

   B. 使他又回到了学校

   C. 使他的病完全好了

7. 方凯没有跟秦悦说再见，因为（　　）

   A. 方凯没有时间

   B. 医生正在给秦悦治病

   C. 方凯太难过了

8. 秦悦对方凯最大的帮助是（　　　）

    A. 帮助他考好试

    B. 让他回到学校

    C. 帮助他勇敢地接受命运的考验

（二）根据课文判断下面句子意思的正误

State whether the following statements are true or false based on the story

1.（　　）方凯觉得癌症没什么大不了的。

2.（　　）秦悦觉得得了癌症以后，最重要的是要想得开。

3.（　　）方凯以为他的病比秦悦重。

4.（　　）秦悦对方凯的影响很大。

5.（　　）方凯病好了以后，考试考得很好。

6.（　　）方凯后悔他没有跟秦悦说再见。

（三）先听故事叙述，然后复述故事

Listen to the narrative first and then retell the story

    在医生告诉方凯他得了癌症的时候，他觉得什么都完了。他觉得癌症就等于死亡，所以他不快乐，甚至不想学习了。有一天，他在医院里认识了一个女孩子，叫秦悦。她是一个高三的学生，虽然得了血癌，但是她认为癌症不一定就等于死亡。得了癌症的人，与其痛不欲生，不如快快乐乐地活着。她约方凯一起复习功课，准备迎接考试，也迎接命运的考验。

    从那以后，方凯变得勇敢了，他的病情也稳定了。现在，方凯每天坐在教室里学习的时候，都会想起这个勇敢的姐姐。

■ 二、词语使用 Application of Vocabulary and Grammar

（一）选择题

Choose the item that is grammatically correct

1. 现在报纸上常说吃蔬菜比吃肉＿＿＿＿＿健康。

    A. 反正　　　　　　　B. 有利于　　　　　　　C. 到底

2. 我每次回家，我朋友都开车送我去机场，我真觉得＿＿＿＿＿。

    A. 用不着　　　　　　B. 没什么大不了　　　　C. 过意不去

3. 我看，你＿＿＿＿＿修这个旧电脑，＿＿＿＿＿买一个新的。

    A. 其实……就……　　　B. 要是……就……

    C. 与其……不如……　　D. 不仅……还要……

4. 他打蓝球打得可好了，我真没有看＿＿＿＿＿他已经五十多岁了。
   A. 起来　　　　　B. 上去　　　　　C. 出来

5. 现在中国什么都有，你去中国＿＿＿＿＿带那么多东西。
   A. 买到了　　　　B. 用不着　　　　C. 用得着

6. 请你把电话号码告诉我，我有事＿＿＿＿＿给你打电话。
   A. 好　　　　　　B. 就　　　　　　C. 只

（二）选择题
Circle the answer that best reflects the meaning of the sentence

1. 比什么有比得病的呀？（　　　）
   A. 没有人跟别人比得病的
   B. 很多人跟别人比得病
   C. 你到底比什么？
   D. 你到底得了什么病？

2. 想开了，也没什么大不了的。（　　　）
   A. 如果你不想你的病，你就没有病了
   B. 如果你不紧张了，你就没有病了
   C. 如果你不怕了，你的病也就不是那么严重的事了
   D. 如果你老想问题，你的问题就很大

3. 天不是还没塌下来吗？地球不是还在转吗？（　　　）
   A. 得了癌症的人感觉地球好像都不转了
   B. 得了癌症，很多事情都不一样了
   C. 得了癌症，每天的生活都停了
   D. 得了癌症，不是什么都完了，我们每天还要做应该做的事情

4. 癌症并不一定就等于死亡。（　　　）
   A. 得了癌症也许可以治好
   B. 癌症跟死不一样
   C. 得了癌症一定得死
   D. 得了癌症绝对能治好

5. 与其痛不欲生，不如争分夺秒、快快乐乐地过好每一天。（　　　）
   A. 每天痛苦地活着，不如每天高高兴兴地做你应该做的事情
   B. 跟每天痛苦地活着的人在一起不会高兴
   C. 为什么痛苦地活着？我们每天都应该高兴

D. 痛苦的人比高兴的人要难相处得多

6. 春天本来就是一首诗摆在你的面前，别跟自己过意不去了。（　　　）

   A. 这首诗就放在你的面前，要是你想看你就看吧

   B. 春天就在你的面前，你不应该在春天觉得难过

   C. 生活像春天一样美好，你不应该因为病而对生活没有希望了

   D. 这首诗就像春天，你看了不应该难过

7. 这本书，我以为再也用不着了……（　　　）

   A. 我觉得这本书我用完了

   B. 我觉得这本书我以后会再用

   C. 我觉得我以后不再需要这本书了

   D. 我觉得这本书没有用了

8. 我真后悔我居然没有叫你一声姐姐。（　　　）

   A. 我真后悔我不好意思叫你一声姐姐

   B. 我真后悔，我应该叫你一声姐姐，可是没有叫

   C. 因为我没有叫你一声姐姐，所以我很后悔

   D. 我也许应该叫你一声姐姐，现在我后悔了

（三）选择适当的词语，改写句中的画线部分

Choose the most appropriate words to replace the underlined parts

A. 过意不去	B. 没有心情	C. 与其……不如……
D. 用不着	E. 也许	F. 到底　　G. 好

1. 现在不下雨了，天气真好，你快点儿把你的功课做完，我们<u>可以</u>出去转转。

2. 上星期我病了，我的同屋送我去医院，跟我在那儿等了两个小时，真让我觉得<u>不好意思</u>。

3. 下午的考试我没考好，现在<u>不想去</u>吃饭，你先去吧。

4. 他这两天没有来上课，打电话也没有人接，<u>真不知道怎么了</u>？

5. 这本书我<u>不用</u>了。你要是有兴趣，可以拿去。

6. A：下个月我要搬出去，得去买一份报纸看租房广告。

   B：你<u>不用</u>看报纸上的广告，上网看广告<u>更好</u>。

7. A：你夏天打算做什么？

   B：还没想好，<u>可能</u>去饭馆儿工作。

（四）用所给词语完成对话

Complete the following dialogues with the items provided in the parenthesis

1. （也许，到底）

A：你今天想学医学，明天想学法学，我真不知道你＿＿＿＿＿想学什么！

B：我＿＿＿＿＿还是学法学。学医学时间太长了！

2. （与其…… 不如……，也许）

A：我看，你＿＿＿＿＿学法学，＿＿＿＿＿学经济。我有很多学经济的朋友大学一毕业就找到了好工作。

B：我再想想，＿＿＿＿＿会学经济。

3. （用不着，好）

A：你赶快去拿行李，我们＿＿＿＿＿去机场，已经有点儿晚了！

B：你＿＿＿＿＿紧张，还有一个多小时呢！

4. （看出来，居然）

A：我昨天去买东西的时候，不知道是谁＿＿＿＿＿找我一张假币！

B：真的吗？你怎么不看仔细点儿呢？

A：你看看，跟真的一样，谁能＿＿＿＿＿啊！

5. （有利于，后悔）

A：我的老师告诉我多听录音＿＿＿＿＿发音。可是我不喜欢听录音，难怪我的发音这么不好，哎，现在＿＿＿＿＿也晚了。

B：你现在听录音还来得及，你一定听说过这句话："Never too late to learn!"

（五）角色扮演 Role play

Make a dialogue with a classmate. One party plays Qin Yue, and the other plays Fang Kai. Your dialogue should incorporate the provided items.

秦悦	方凯
You have heard that a teenage boy, who is also a cancer patient, was just admitted to your ward, and he is very sad and depressed. You have decided to cheer him up and help him face the challenge.	You feel very sad and frustrated—How come life is so unfair: Why does it have to be you? The cancer diagnosis killed your future. Then in comes this girl with a big smile on her face. Who is she?

1. 出去转转	1. 没心情
2. 其实	2. 癌症＝死亡
3. 没什么大不了的	3. 不想参加中考
4. 与其……不如……	4. 用不着了
5. 咱俩一起……	5. 男子汉说话算话
6. 不仅……还……	
7. 男子汉可要说话算话	

■ 三、课堂讨论 Discussion

1. 为什么秦悦得了癌症还很快乐？

2. 秦悦约方凯一起复习功课是为了什么？

3. 秦悦是怎么帮助方凯改变了对生活的看法的？

第十三课 箱 子

A Trunk

编剧：张濯夕

人物 （Characters）

大李（Dà Lǐ）——男，二十二岁。

小赵（Xiǎo Zhào）——男，十九岁。

箱包老板（xiāngbāo lǎobǎn）——男，三十五岁。

课 文 Text

大　李：少花钱多**办事**，对于你来说是有点难度，可对于我小菜一碟[N1]，不就一只箱子吗?[N2] 兄弟，保证你三十块钱拿下[N3]，怎么样?

1. 箱子	xiāngzi	n.	chest; box; case; trunk
2. 箱包	xiāngbāo	n.	cases; bags
3. 办事	bàn shì	vo.	handle affairs; do things
4. 难度	nándù	n.	degree of difficulty
5. 小菜一碟	xiǎocài yì dié		a piece of cake (literally：a dishful of vegetable)
6. 拿下	ná xià	vc.	capture; seize (also see note 3)

小　赵：**好嘞**！

大　李：哎，对了，待会儿买箱子的时候你可别**吱声**，瞧我的。

小　赵：得嘞。

大　李：走吧。

老　板：怎么着？**哥**儿**俩**买箱子啊？

大　李：便宜点儿我们就来一个。

老　板：我这箱子包你便宜，五十块钱，你拿走，别**回头**，**不然**我
　　　　后悔。

大　李：别逗了[N4]，五十块？我说，你多少天没**开张**了？可**逮**着我
　　　　们了是不是——**顶多**三十。

老　板：我说**老弟**，我这箱子昨天刚上的**货**，四十五，你就让我挣
　　　　五块钱还不行啊。

大　李：就这个**数**，你要是不卖，我们**扭头**就走。

老　板：就这个数，你拿走。

7.	好嘞	hǎo lei		alright
8.	吱声	zī shēng	vo.	speak (colloq.)
9.	哥儿俩	gēr liǎ		two buddies
10.	回头	huí tóu	vo.	turn round; look back; trun back
11.	不然	bùrán	conj.	otherwise
12.	开张	kāizhāng	v.	open for business
13.	逮	dǎi	v.	catch; get hold of
14.	顶多	dǐng duō		at most
15.	老弟	lǎodì	n.	young fellow (a form of address for a male adult younger than oneself)
16.	货	huò	n.	goods; commodity
17.	数	shù	n.	figure; number
18.	扭头	niǔ tóu	vo.	turn around

大　李：我说啊，你这个人怎么那么**死性**啊？得，四十就四十[N5]，见过钱没有？[N6]赵儿[N7]，给他钱。

小　赵：哥，四十是不是有些太贵了？

大　李：不贵，我看这货还行。

小　赵：老板，这箱子我们要了，给你钱。哎，把钱放**信封**里，哪儿去了？

大　李：得得得，我先给你**垫上**，来，**找钱**。

老　板：五十，找您十块。

大　李：行，就这么着[N8]。

老　板：**走好**啊。

小　赵：大李哥。

大　李：哎。

小　赵：你不是说这箱子三十就能拿下么？

大　李：就这箱子，**嘿嘿**，兄弟别说四十，就是六十也**值**了，你呀，就偷着乐吧[N9]。哎，对了[N10]，一会儿啊，好好检查检查里边，啊。该**上岗**了，我呢，先过去，别**迟到**了，快点儿啊。

19.	死性	sǐxing	adj.	stubborn
20.	信封	xìnfēng	n.	envelope
21.	垫上	diàn shang	vc.	pay for someone and get reimbursed later
22.	找钱	zhǎo qián	vo.	give the change
23.	走好	zǒu hǎo	vc.	bye (literally: walk carefully)
24.	么	me	p.	(question-end particle equivalent to 吗)
25.	嘿嘿	hēihēi	ono.	(onomatopoeia for the sound of laughter)
26.	值	zhí	v.	be worth
27.	上岗	shàng gǎng	vo.	take over a shift; begin to work
28.	迟到	chídào	v.	be late; arrive late

小　赵：哎。

大　李：**抓紧点**儿**时间**。

小　赵：大李哥，我觉得咱们这箱子的事儿做得不太合适，你看人
　　　　家**做买卖**也不太容易⋯⋯

大　李：你这人啊，真有意思，我还以为你得谢谢我呢。要是别人
　　　　啊，乐还来不及呢，你倒好，当成**心病**了。你要（是）不
　　　　要也成，给我啊。我啊正想买一箱子呢。

小　赵：大李哥，这箱子你要是真想要，那我就送给您，不过这钱
　　　　啊，得给人家送过去。

大　李：**得了**，这儿不是咱们老家，你知道这些**买卖人**一天挣多少
　　　　钱吗？他们**手指头缝里漏**出一点儿，就够你活**一辈子**[N11]了。

小　赵：那挣多少钱也是人家（的）钱啊，跟咱没关系，大李哥，
　　　　下了班以后你就跟我去一趟，把这箱子还给人家。

大　李：看见没有，不用我**陪**你去啦，人家找上门来了[N12]，到嘴的
　　　　鸭子飞啦[N13]。

29.	抓紧(点儿)时间	zhuā jǐn (diǎnr) shíjiān		make good use of the time
30.	做买卖	zuò mǎimai	vo.	do business
31.	心病	xīnbìng	n.	worry; anxiety
32.	得了	dé le	v.	enough of it (used to stop the other personfrom continuing to say or do something)
33.	买卖人	mǎimairén	n.	businessman
34.	手指头	shǒuzhítou	n.	finger(colloq.)
35.	缝里	fèng li		chink
36.	漏	lòu	v.	leak; let out
37.	一辈子	yí bèizi		all one's life; a lifetime
38.	陪	péi	v.	accompany

老　板：小哥儿俩，真在这儿当**保安**哪？

老　板：我说你们俩可真够**马虎**的……

小　赵：哟，大哥，是我们马虎还是您马虎啊？您看这事，我们正**琢磨**着找你去呢。

老　板：甭找我，我知道你们着急。你看，我这在**摊**儿上捡的，我看这里头又是证件又是钱的[N14]，我想啊，可能是你们俩谁的。

小　赵：哟，真是我（的），大哥，**怪不得**刚才买箱子的时候我找不着呢，**敢情**[N15]这是**掉**您**摊**儿上了。太谢谢了。

老　板：哎呀，小伙子，这以后多**注点**儿**意**啊。

39.	保安	bǎo'ān	n.	security guard
40.	马虎	mǎhu	adj.	careless；negligent
41.	琢磨	zuómo	v.	ponder；figure out a way
42.	摊儿	tānr	n.	stall；stand
43.	怪不得	guàibude		no wonder；so that's why
44.	敢情	gǎnqing		(see note 15)
45.	掉	diào	v.	drop；fall
46.	注(点儿)意	zhù (diǎnr) yì	v.	be careful；pay attention

小　赵：哎，您不是为这箱子来的？

老　板：箱子？箱子怎么了？

小　赵：哎哟，您看这事闹的[N16]，您看。

老　板：哎哟，你瞧我这脑子，昨天刚上的货，还没来得及**拆封**呢，我们**一般**进箱子，都是大箱子套小箱子，你看看，哎哟，看来我真得感谢你们呀，谢谢，**多谢**了，多谢了。

大　李：你们俩呀，就别谢了，这叫**缘分**呐！

47. 拆封	chāi fēng	vo.	tear open the seal
48. 一般	yìbān	adj.	usually
49. 多谢	duō xiè		many thanks; thanks a lot
50. 缘分	yuánfèn	n.	predestined affinity; fate

注释　Notes

1. "小菜一碟"：

"小菜一碟"是"一碟小菜"的意思，比喻很容易做到的事情。口语。

The colloquial term "小菜一碟" literally mean "a dishful of pickled vegetable". It serves as a metaphor for something easy to do.

（1）对于你来说是有点儿难度，可对于我小菜一碟。

It may be difficult to you，but for me it's only a piece of cake.

（2）这件事小菜一碟，你不必担心。

This matter is just a piece of cake，and you don't have to worry.

2. "不就一只箱子吗"：

这是一个反问句：不是只是一个箱子吗？意思是：只是一个箱子。

This is a rhetorical question. It suggests that it is nothing more than a case.

3. "拿下"：

意思是：把问题解决了，战胜了对手等等。口语。

As a colloquial expression，"拿下" means "to solve a problem" or "to subdue an adversary".

（1）兄弟保证你三十块钱拿下，怎么样？

I guarantee that you can get it for thirty dollars，OK？

（2）这场比赛我们队肯定拿下了。

Our team will definitely take this game.

（3）那个案子你一定要拿下！

You absolutely have to crack that case！

4. "别逗了"：

意思是：别开玩笑了。口语。

This colloquial formula literally means "No more joking." It is often used to express one's disbelief of what the other person has just said.

（1）老板：我这箱子包你便宜，五十块钱，你拿走，别回头，不然我后悔。

The owner：I assure you this case is inexpensive，only fifty dollars. You can take it, but then don't turn around, otherwise I'd regret.

大李：别逗了，五十块？我说你多少天没开张了？可逮着我们了是不是——顶多三十。

Da Li：Fifty bucks? You must be kidding. Perhaps you had no business for many days and now want to extort money from us? It should be no more than thirty.

（2）A：你考试得了 100 分，你知道吗？

You got one hundred points for your exam, do you know?

B：你别逗了，我已经拿到考卷了，才 80 分。

You kidding! I got my exam paper back already. It was only eighty.

5. "四十就四十"：

意思是：你说四十就（给你）四十吧。口语。

This colloquialism expresses a reluctant acceptance of what the other person has just proposed：Since you insist on forty, I will go by that figure.

6. "见过钱没有"：

这是个反问句，意思是：你没有看见过钱吧？（所以你把钱看得这么重）。

This is a rhetorical question asked in a sarcastic tone：Perhaps you have never seen money, and that's why money is so dear to you.

7. "赵儿"（Zhàor）：

叫一个熟人时，可以只叫他的姓，但是姓要儿化。这个叫法跟叫"小赵"一样。口语。

When addressing an acquaintance by his surname only, the syllable for the surname must be suffixed with the r sound，e. g. , Zhaor. The address of "Zhaor" is roughly interchangeable with "Xiao Zhao" (Young Zhao)，but the latter form is much more common.

8. "就这么着"：

"这么着"的意思是"这样"，参见第一课注释 3。"就这么着"念做 jiù zhèmezhāo，意思是"就这样"，表示同意对方的意见。口语。

"这么着" is another way to say "这样". See also note 3 in Lesson 1. The phrase "就这么着" is pronounced "jiù zhèmezhāo". As a colloquialism，it denotes the speaker's agreement to the other person's proposal.

9. "你呀，就偷着乐吧"：

Go ahead to rejoice behind your closed doors.

当一个人拣到了便宜，不便于公开说出来，别人可以这样说他。口语。
再如：

When someone has gained an advantage and doesn't want it to be known to others, this colloquial formula can be used to mock him. Another example：

(1) 他以为花钱不多，就买到了真古董，正一个人在家偷着乐呢。

He thought he had bought a genuine antique for a low price, and was making merry all by himself at home.

10. "对了"：

一个人突然想起来什么事情，可以说"对了……"。

When one suddenly recalls something that was almost forgotten，"对了" is often used.

(1) 就是六十也值了，你呀，就偷着乐吧。哎，对了，一会儿啊，好好检查检查里面啊。

It's worth even sixty. You can celebrate behind your closed doors. Oh yeah，in a few moments you should check the inside carefully.

(2) 对了，小张，那天我交给你的那篇文章呢？我想看看。

Oh，Xiao Zhang，where is the article that I gave you the other day? I'd like to read it.

(3) 你走吧。对了，等等，小李让你去他那儿一趟。

You may go now. Oh yes，just a moment，Xiao Li wanted you to go to see him.

11. "他们手指缝里漏一点儿，就够你活一辈子"：

They let go a little bit between their fingers and it would be enough for your whole life.

这句话的意思是说"他们"很有钱。口语。

This is a colloquial expression that heightens the disparity between the rich and the poor.

12. "人家找上门来了"：

They've come knocking at the door.

"人家"指别人。"找上门"指因为做错了事、欠别人的钱物等，别人到家里来讲道理、讨还钱物。口语。

The term "人家" refers to a certain person or a certain group of people. "找上门" is a colloquial formula to refer to what happens in a dispute：

that the victim goes to the door of the guilty party to reason things out or to ask for a compensation. e. g. :

(1) 看见没有，不用我陪你去啦，瞧见没有，人家找上门来了。

Look，I needn't go with you any more. Don't you see? They are here knocking at the door.

(2) 你家的孩子打破了邻居的窗户，邻居找上门来了。

Your child broke your neighbors' window，and they are now at your door.

(3) 你既然知道打人不对，就主动去跟人家道歉吧，不要等人家找上门来。

Since you know it was wrong for you to hit him，you should go to apologize to him，and not wait for him to come knocking at your door.

13. **"到嘴的鸭子飞啦"**：

The duck flew away between the teeth.

比喻得到了又失去了，也说"煮熟的鸭子飞了"。口语。

This is a colloquialism that metaphorically refers to a situation in which one loses between cup and lip or fails when victory is almost secured. It also takes the other form "煮熟的鸭子飞了" (The duck flew away from the dining table).

14. **"我看里头又是证件又是钱的……"**：

I saw both ID's and money in it...

这里的"是"表示存在的意思。

Here the verb "是" means "to exist".

15. **"敢情"**：

表示发现了以前没有发现的情况。口语。"原来"也有这样的用法。

"敢情" is a colloquial term to be used to introduce something the speaker did not see preciously but has just come to see. In this sense it is similar to "原来"，which is the regular and more commonly used term.

(1) 怪不得刚才买箱子的时候我找不着呢，敢情这是掉（到）您（的）摊儿上了。

No wonder I couldn't find it when I was buying the case a moment ago. Who would have thought I dropped it at your stall.

(2) 我说你们俩怎么长得这么像呢，敢情你们是兄弟呀。

I was wondering why the two of you looked so alike. You guys turn out to be brothers!

（3）我找了你半天了，敢情你躲在这儿玩儿游戏机呢。

I've been looking for you for a long time，and so you have been hiding here and playing games on the machine.

16. **"您看这事闹的"**：

You see，what a mess！

这句话的意思类似：事情怎么会这样。表示说话人没有想到事情会这样，有时有抱歉、后悔的意味。

The sentence suggests that the situation has developed in such a way that is beyond the speaker's expectation and out of his or her control. It is often said in an apologetic tone.

听说练习 Listening & Speaking Exercises

■ **一、课文理解 Text Comprehension**

（一）根据故事情节选择适当的答案

Please choose the most appropriate answer based on the story

1. 小赵，待会儿买箱子的时候你可别<u>吱声</u>，瞧我的。（　　）
   A. 别说话　　　　　B. 别回答　　　　　C. 要安静

2. 我这箱子包你便宜，五十块钱，<u>你拿走，别回头</u>，不然我后悔。
   　　　　　　　　　　　　　　　　　　　　　　　　（　　）
   A. 不卖了　　　　　B. 快买了吧　　　　C. 卖错了

3. 顶多三十，就这个数，你要是不卖，我们<u>扭头就走</u>。（　　）
   A. 受骗了　　　　　B. 生气了　　　　　C. 不买了

4. 小赵觉得这箱子的事儿他们<u>做得不太合适</u>。（　　）
   A. 说话太不客气了
   B. 不应该这样做
   C. 买得太便宜了

5. 赵儿，你这人啊，真有意思，我还以为你得谢谢我呢，要是别人啊，乐还来不及呢，你倒好，当成<u>心病</u>了。（　　）
   A. 以为心病　　　　B. 发愁的事　　　　C. 让心病

（二）根据课文判断下面句子意思的正误

State whether the following statements are true or false based on the story

1. （　　）少花钱多办事，对于大李来说有点儿难度，可对于小赵来说是小菜一碟。

2. （　　）小赵买的箱子值六十块钱。

3. （　　）箱子买得很便宜使小赵越想越高兴。

4. （　　）大李认为像卖箱子这样的买卖人非常有钱。

5. （　　）卖箱子的老板找上门来把小赵买的箱子又拿回去了。

6. （　　）小赵发现他买的箱子里面又有证件又有很多钱。

（三）先听故事叙述，然后复述故事

Listen to the narrative first and then retell the story

　　小赵和朋友大李一起去买箱子。大李认为小赵在讨价还价上不如他，所以要小赵在买箱子时别吱声，看他的。

　　小赵看上了一只箱子，卖箱子的老板说他的箱子最便宜，五十元，卖这个箱子他只挣五块钱。大李说他要这个价是开玩笑，在他看来，这个箱子顶多值三十。两人说来说去，最后箱子用四十元买了下来。

　　小赵付钱时发现找不到钱了。大李帮他垫上钱，他们提着箱子就走了。

　　后来小赵打开箱子发现里边还有一个小箱子。这卖箱子的人当时不知道。他觉得心里很不安，认为应该把这个小箱子还给卖箱子的人。大李却认为那些买卖人比他们有钱得多，不必这么做。

　　正说着，他们看见卖箱子的老板跑过来了。他们以为老板是为那个小箱子来的。没想到老板是给他们送小赵丢的钱的。装钱的信封里除了钱还有证件。小赵很感动，连说谢谢，同时也把小箱子还给了老板。

二、词语使用 Application of Vocabulary and Grammar

（一）选择题

Choose the item that is grammatically correct

1. 不就一只箱子吗？兄弟保证你三十块钱拿_____，怎么样？

　　A. 到　　　　　B. 走　　　　　C. 下　　　　　D. 来

2. A：要不要买箱子？

　　B：便宜点儿我们就_____一个。

　　A. 给　　　　　B. 送　　　　　C. 看　　　　　D. 来

3. 你找不到钱，我先给你垫_____，来，是四十块钱。

　　A. 到　　　　　B. 好　　　　　C. 下　　　　　D. 上

4. 哥，四十是不是有些_____贵了？

　　A. 很　　　　　B. 太　　　　　C. 特别　　　　　D. 非常

5. 就这箱子，嘿嘿，兄弟别说四十，就是六十_____值了。

　　A. 够　　　　　B. 更　　　　　C. 也　　　　　D. 就

6. 他挣多少钱也是人家的钱啊，_____咱没关系，大李哥，下了班以后你就跟我去一趟，把这箱子还给人家。

A. 都　　　　　B. 只　　　　　C. 跟　　　　　D. 对

7. 哟，怪不得 _____ 买箱子的时候我找不着呢，敢情这是掉您摊儿上了。太谢谢了。

A. 从前　　　　B. 以前　　　　C. 刚才　　　　D. 待会

8. 你看，我这在摊儿上捡的，我看里头 _____ 证件 _____ 钱的，我想啊，可能是你们俩谁的。

A. 不但……而且……　　　　B. 也……也……
C. 不是……就是……　　　　D. 又是……又是……

（二）选择题

Circle the answer that best reflects the meaning of the underlined portion of the sentence

1. 别逗了，五十块？我说你多少天没开张了？（　　）
   A. 没开门了
   B. 没人来了
   C. 没说话了
   D. 没卖出东西了

2. 我这箱子包你便宜，五十块钱你去哪儿都买不到。（　　）
   A. 保证便宜
   B. 你包便宜
   C. 不包便宜
   D. 打包便宜

3. 我们一般进箱子，都是大箱子套小箱子，看来我真得感谢你们呀，多谢了。（　　）
   A. 大小箱子很多
   B. 大箱子在小箱子外边
   C. 小箱子在大箱子外边
   D. 很多箱子放在一起

4. 哟，大哥，是我们马虎还是您马虎啊？您把钱包掉我摊儿上了。
   　　　　　　　　　　　　　　　　　　　　　　　　（　　）

A. 我们马虎　　　　　　　B. 您马虎
C. 一方马虎　　　　　　　D. 都不马虎

（三）选择适当的词语，替换句中的画线部分

Choose the most appropriate words to replace the underlined parts

| A. 敢情　　B. 小菜一碟　　　C. 正偷着乐呢　　　　D. 找上门来 |
| E. 拿下　　F. 不就一只箱子吗　　G. 手指缝里漏出一点　　H. 别逗了 |

1. 只是一个箱子，又不是冰箱，能要那么多钱吗？

2. 这件事对于他来说是有点儿难度，可对你来说是很容易做到的。

3. 她父母那么有钱，随便给她一点就够她活一辈子的了。

4. 这场足球赛我们队肯定会赢！

5. A：这次考试，你全班第一！

　　B：别开玩笑了，我是全班倒数第一。

6. 二十元就买了一个皮箱，他嘴上不说心里可高兴了。

7. 你既然知道偷东西不对，就主动去公安局认错吧，不要等警察到你家找你。

8. 我说你们俩怎么长得这么像呢，原来你们是姐妹呀。

（四）用所给词语完成对话

Complete the following dialogues with the items provided in the parenthesis

1. （小菜一碟，别逗了，拿下，死性）

　　A：这辆旧自行车还不错，不知六十块钱能不能_____？

　　B：你这么会说话，这种事对你来说还不是_____。

　　A：_____，这个买车的特_____，跟他打交道可不容易。

2. （到嘴的鸭子飞啦，敢情，你看，）

　　大李：看见没有，卖给我们箱子的那个人来了。看来，_____。

　　老板：我在找你们呐，_____我这在摊儿上捡的，我看里头又是证件又是钱的，我想啊，可能是你们俩谁的。

　　大李：太谢谢了。

　　小赵：这世界上_____还有这么好的人呐！

3. （对了，你看这事闹的）

　　张大哥：你怎么买菜买了几个钟头？

　　张大嫂：没想到我这身打扮他们把我当成精神病人了！把我带进市场管理办公室，不让我走。

　　张大哥：_____。_____，你买的鱼呢？

　　张大嫂：没买成。忘了带钱。

（五）角色扮演 Role play

Make a dialogue with a classmate. One party plays Laoban，and the other plays Da Li. The two are bargaining over the price of a suitcase. Your dialogue should incorporate the provided items.

老板	大李
You see two young men looking at your suitcases，you greet them and try to encourage them to buy. You promise them the lowest possible price that you might regret later. You happily say bye to them after they purchased a case from you.	You help your friend Xiao Zhao to buy a suitcase. You tell the seller you'd buy it only if the price is cheap. You'd walk away if the seller would not sell it for 30 *yuan*. You accuse the seller of being stubborn. You eventually buy the case for 40 *yuan*.
1. 怎么着　　2. 哥儿俩 3. 包你便宜　4. 别回头 5. 后悔　　　6. 刚上的货 7. 还不行啊　8. 走好	1. 便宜　　　2. 别逗了 3. 没开张　　4. 逮着我们 5. 顶多　　　6. 扭头就走 7. 死性　　　8. Nu. 就 Nu.

■ **三、课堂讨论 Discussion**

1. 卖箱子的老板说："我这箱子包你便宜，五十块钱，你拿走，别回头，不然我后悔。"这句话什么意思？他为什么会后悔？

2. 小赵为什么觉得这箱子的事儿他们做得不太合适？

3. 像卖箱子的老板那样的人多吗？为什么？

4. 要是卖箱子的老板没来找他们，小赵会去找老板把小箱子还给他吗？为什么？

第十四课 尴尬的礼品

A Present

 编剧：尤欣

人物（Characters）

小张（Xiǎo Zhāng）——某公司技术人员。

李梅（Lǐ Méi）——小张的妻子。

王经理（Wáng jīnglǐ）

课 文 Text

李 梅：回来了？快洗手吃饭吧。

小 张：等会儿再吃，我先跟你说个事儿……

李 梅：什么事啊？你可别吓唬我呀。

小 张：我们公司啊马上要上一个**设计项目**，经理让**所有**技术人员

---

1. 尴尬	gāngà	adj.	awkward；embarrassing
2. 礼品	lǐpǐn	n.	gift；present
3. 人员	rényuán	n.	personnel；staff
4. 设计	shèjì	v.	design；plan
5. 项目	xiàngmù	n.	project；program
6. 所有	suǒyǒu	adj.	all

都参加**竞标**，一旦[N1]**中标**就能**独立**设计。

李　梅：真的？这可是好事呀！你不是一直想自己独立设计吗？你
赶紧去竞标啊。

小　张：我也得**竞**得上呀。公司那么多技术人员，还都净是**博士、
硕士**的，天上掉**馅儿饼**[N2]也**轮不到**我这个**学士**头上。

李　梅：你们经理对你印象怎么样？

小　张：什么意思？

李　梅：咳，我的意思是啊，你们经理要是对你印象不**深**的话，咱
们就得**送礼**——也许人家不在乎咱们送什么东西，但重要
的是**感情**，我的**傻**学士！

小　张：你这太**俗**了吧？

李　梅：你这人，想吃鱼还怕**腥**[N3]啊？你看，这不是现成的吗？

小　张：这哪儿来的？

7. 竞标	jìng biāo	vo.	competitive bidding
8. 一旦	yídàn	adv.	in case (something happens)；once
9. 中标	zhòng biāo	vo.	get (or win) the bid
10. 独立	dúlì	adj.	independent；on one's own
11. 竞	jìng	v.	compete；contest
12. 博士	bóshì	n.	Ph. D.；doctor's degree
13. 硕士	shuòshì	n.	Master's degree (of Arts or Science)
14. 馅儿饼	xiànrbǐng	n.	pancake；pie
15. 轮不到	lún bu dào	vc.	it (usu. a good thing) won't come one's way
16. 学士	xuéshì	n.	bachelor's degree
17. 深	shēn	adj.	deep；profound
18. 送礼	sòng lǐ	vo.	give a present；present a gift (to sb.)
19. 感情	gǎnqíng	n.	feeling；affection
20. 傻	shǎ	adj.	stupid；foolish
21. 俗	sú	adj.	vulgar；in poor taste
22. 腥	xīng	adj.	fishy (smell)

李　梅：你妈今天来了，说你这两天工作紧张又爱**失眠**，让你补身体的。

小　张：人家都是儿子给父母买**补品**，这倒好，颠了个儿[N4]。得，明天**抽时间**给我妈送回去。

李　梅：别价[N5]呀，咱们先拿它**应急**，回头给你妈送更好的还不行？听我的，咱们现在吃饭，吃完饭就去。

小　张：行了，反正东西也送出去了！

李　梅：你呀就等好**消息**吧。

小　张：喂，哦，妈……东西我看见了……我都说了我身体挺好的，您还买什么东西呀！……什么？里面有一张**纸条**？我

23.	失眠	shīmián	v.	suffer from insomnia
24.	补品	bǔpǐn	n.	tonic
25.	抽时间	chōu shíjiān	vo.	manage to find time
26.	应急	yìng jí	vo.	meet an emergency; meet an urgent need
27.	消息	xiāoxi	n.	news
28.	纸条	zhǐtiáo	n.	paper strip; scrip

没看见啊？您都写什么了？……哎呀，您可真是的，这下麻烦了。我回头[N6]再跟您说吧，妈，再见！

李　梅：什么麻烦了？

小　张：都怪你，非急着送吧，这下倒好了[N7]，我妈生怕我不吃，在盒里面夹了张纸条。

李　梅：写什么了？

小　张：写什么了！"儿子，你可千万[N8]要想着吃，好好补身体。"

李　梅：你妈真这么写了……

李　梅：怎么样？

小　张：还能怎么样？竞标结果出来了，没有我！……

李　梅：没有就没有嘛，咱们啊，下回努力！

小　张：你以为这就完事了？明天经理要找我谈话……

李　梅：谈什么？

小　张：谈什么？！谈"感情"呗！都管人家叫儿子了，能没"感情"吗？公司正在裁员呢，我这不是自己往枪口上撞吗？[N9]

李　梅：那怎么办？

小　张：唉。

29.	真是的	zhēn shì de		you are too much (as used in this story)
30.	盒	hé	n.	box
31.	夹	jiā	v.	put in between
32.	千万	qiānwàn	adv.	by all means; absolutely; (of an admonition) must
33.	结果	jiéguǒ	n. /conj.	result; outcome
34.	努力	nǔlì	adj. /v.	make efforts; try hard
35.	完事	wán shì		come to an end
36.	谈话	tán huà	vo.	discuss; talk
37.	裁员	cái yuán	vo.	cut staff; lay off employees
38.	枪口	qiāngkǒu	n.	gun (also see note 9)
39.	撞	zhuàng	v.	bump against (see note 9)

（画外音：请进。）

小　张：经理，您找我？

王经理：哦，小张啊，来来来，坐坐坐！小张，今天来是想跟你说件事，从下星期开始，你就不要来公司了……

小　张：别价，经理，上回送礼的事，那是我不对，您可千万别**误会**……

王经理：你不说我倒给忘了，这个你拿回去，那天我不在家，你们走得急，我**爱人**又没**追上**你们。

小　张：我……

王经理：别说了，这事啊我知道。其实这次项目的事，公司是**经过**认真**研究讨论**而**决定**的，你嘛，还年轻，以后**有的是**这样的机会。现在嘛，对你来说最重要的就是学习，正好，公司有一个到**特区考察**的**名额**，我们认真研究了一下，无论从年龄上还有工作表现上，你去最合适，所以公司决定**派**你去。

小　张：经理，原来……您不是要炒我啊。

40. 误会	wùhuì	v.	misunderstand
41. 爱人	àiren	n.	spouse；husband or wife
42. 追上	zhuī shang	vc.	catch up（with sb.）
43. 经过	jīngguò	v./n.	based on；as a result of
44. 研究	yánjiū	v.	consider；deliberate
45. 讨论	tǎolùn	v./n.	discuss；discussion
46. 决定	juédìng	v.	decide
47. 有的是	yǒu de shì		quite a lot；plenty
48. 特区	tèqū	n.	special zone；special（administrative）region
49. 考察	kǎochá	v.	inspect；observe and study
50. 名额	míng'é	n.	quota of people
51. 派	pài	v.	send；dispatch

王经理：炒你？像你这么**年轻有为**的**技术员**，公司留还怕留不住
　　　　呢！[N10] 好好干吧，年轻人，公司的未来可就**靠**你们了！

小　张：是，我会努力的。

52.	年轻有为	niánqīng yǒuwéi		young and promising
53.	技术员	jìshùyuán	n.	technician
54.	靠	kào	v.	depend on；rely on

注释 Notes

1. "一旦":

副词"一旦"表示一个不确定的时间，用于出现了一种新的情况。这种新情况可能已经出现。

"一旦", adverb, indicates an indefinite point of time at which a new situation occurs. The situation could have already taken place.

(1) 他们结婚十几年了，一旦离婚了，感情上还是有些不舍的。

They were married for ten some years, and were a bit loath to part from each other when they first divorced.

更常用于没有发生的情况。

However, "一旦" is more frequently used with an unrealized situation.

(2) 经理让所有技术人员都参加竞标，一旦中标就能独立设计。

The manager asked all the technical personnel to compete for the project. Once you win, you will be allowed to design the project independently.

(3) 他找工作找得太累了，他想，一旦找到工作了，一定好好休息几天。

He's so burned out from job-hunting. Once he finds one, he hopes to take a couple of days' break.

2. "天上掉馅儿饼":

意思是：没有做任何事情，而得到了意想不到的好处。

"Good fortune falls into one's lap." This expression indicates that one receives good results without making any efforts.

(1) 公司里那么多技术人员，还都净是博士、硕士的，天上掉馅儿饼也轮不到我这个学士头上。

Our company is full of engineers and technicians, all with Master's degrees or Ph. D's. Even if there were such thing as a free lunch, it would never come my way because I've only got a bachelor's degree.

(2) 成功要靠自己的努力，没有天上掉馅儿饼的好事。

Success comes with one's hard work. You can't find money growing on trees.

(3) 那个大公司来找你去工作，这是天上掉馅儿饼的好事，你怎么还不想去？

That huge corporation offered you a job—that's a free, once-in-a-life-time opportunity. Why don't you want to take it?

3. **"想吃鱼还怕腥啊"：**

这是个反问句。鱼好吃，可是有腥味。如果一个人遇到一件能给自己带来好处的事情，可是这件事可能又会给自己带来麻烦，所以就会犹豫，就可以说："想吃鱼还怕腥啊？"这句话的意思是：想得到好处就不要怕事情可能会给自己带来麻烦。

This is a rhetorical question. Fish is tasty, but it stinks (as all fish do). The expression "想吃鱼还怕腥啊?" is used here to suggest that if one wants the benefit of something, one should also expect the disadvantages that come along with the benefit.

4. **"人家都是儿子给父母买补品，这倒好，颠了个儿"：**

"这倒好"是一句反话，实际意思是"这不好"。"颠了个儿"意思是颠倒过来了：别人都是儿子给父母买东西，现在是我父母给我买东西。

"这倒好" is said here in an ironic sense. The speaker actually means "This is bad." "颠了个儿" means "the opposite": The tradition is that the younger generation gives presents to their elders (to show filial piety), whereas now my parents give me presents.

5. **"别价"：**

见第二课注释16。口语。

"别价", see note 16 in Lesson 2.

6. **"回头"：**

过一段时间，和"以后"意思接近，但一般来说这段时间不会太长。口语。

"回头", a colloquial usage, meaning "in a little while", similar to "以后".

(1) 这件事有点儿麻烦。我回头再跟您说吧！

This is a bit complicated, I will tell you later.

(2) 工作证找不到了？别着急，先吃饭，回头我帮你找。

You can't find your employee's ID? Don't worry. You have your meal, and I'll help you look for it after eating.

(3) 这件事你别告诉他，他知道了，回头一定会来找你的麻烦。

Don't tell him about this. Once he knows, he will definitely take it out on you later.

7. **"这下倒好了"**:

这也是一句反话，意思是：这下子（发生这件事以后）麻烦（不好）了。

This is a sarcastic remark. The speaker means "there will be trouble ahead".

8. **"千万"**:

意思是"一定"，表示恳切地叮嘱、嘱咐，要对方一定要注意。用于祈使句。

"千万" means "must" or "at all cost". It is usually used when earnestly reminding someone (not) to do something, therefore, it always appears in an imperative sentence.

(1) 儿子，你可千万要想着吃，好好补身体。

Son, you must remember to eat it to improve your health.

(2) 那个地方很危险，你千万要注意。

That place is very dangerous, you must be careful at all costs.

(3) 到了那里千万给妈妈打个电话。

You must call mom when you get there.

9. **"我这不是自己往枪口上撞吗"**:

这是一个反问句，意思是：自己主动送死、找死。

This is a rhetorical question meaning "Isn't that asking for trouble?"

10. **"公司还怕留不住你们呢"**:

意思是：公司怕你们离开，去别的地方工作。

The company is afraid that you will leave it for a better job.

听说练习　Listening & Speaking Exercises

■ **一、课文理解 Text Comprehension**

（一）根据故事情节选择适当的答案
Please choose the most appropriate answer based on the story

1. 小张很想（　　）
    A. 独立设计　　　　　　B. 参加竞标　　　　　C. 给经理送礼

2. 小张觉得自己竞不上这个项目，因为（　　）
    A. 经理对他的印象不深
    B. 公司里的技术员博士、硕士很多
    C. 上面的两个答案都对

3. 小张的学位是（　　）
    A. 学士　　　　　　　　B. 硕士　　　　　　　C. 博士

4. 小张的妻子认为送礼是为了（　　）
    A. 让收礼人喜欢你的礼物
    B. 让收礼人补身体
    C. 让收礼人对你有感情

5. 礼物是（　　）
    A. 李梅特地买的
    B. 小张特地买的
    C. 小张的妈妈给小张买的

6. 礼物送出去以后，小张才知道（　　）
    A. 礼物不太好看
    B. 礼物盒里夹了一张妈妈给他写的纸条
    C. 礼物太便宜

7. 公司经理决定（　　）
    A. 把小张裁了　　　　B. 让小张去特区考察　　C. 让小张中标

8. 公司经理认为小张以后（　　）

　　A. 对公司会很重要　　　B. 需要学习　　　　　　C. 不应该送礼

（二）根据课文判断下面句子意思的正误

State whether the following statements are true or false based on the story

1.（　　）小张认为学士学历在他的公司太低。

2.（　　）李梅觉得送礼有利于加深别人对你的印象。

3.（　　）李梅让小张用他妈妈的礼物因为他们不想花钱买礼物。

4.（　　）小张的妈妈对小张的身体不放心。

5.（　　）王经理让他爱人收了小张的礼物。

6.（　　）王经理看到了小张的妈妈给小张写的纸条。

7.（　　）王经理对小张的印象很好，这跟礼物没有关系。

8.（　　）公司要送小张去特区考察。

（三）先听故事叙述，然后复述故事

Listen to the narrative first and then retell the story

　　小张他们公司有一个重要的设计项目，大家都想做，小张当然也想做。公司经理让大家竞标，谁中标谁就做这个项目。小张觉得自己的希望不大，因为他只是学士，而公司的大多数技术人员不是硕士就是博士。小张的妻子李梅让他给经理送礼，说这样经理会对他有好印象。于是他们就把小张的妈妈送给小张的一盒补品送给了经理。没想到小张妈妈在补品盒里留了一张纸条，说："儿子，你可千万要想着吃，好好补补身体。"小张后悔死了！他想，公司现在正在裁员，我管经理叫"儿子"，经理一定会把我裁了。可是经理根本没有打开礼物，他把礼物还给了小张。他还决定送小张去特区考察，这当然不是因为他送礼，而是因为他工作表现好。

二、词语使用 Application of Vocabulary and Grammar

（一）选择题

Choose the item that is grammatically correct

1. 我们学校明年要_____一个在中国的留学项目，听说是在上海。

　　A. 中标　　　　B. 下　　　　　C. 上　　　　　D. 竞标

2. 虽然我只见过他一次，但是我_____他的印象很深，常常想起他。

　　A. 对　　　　　B. 给　　　　　C. 跟　　　　　D. 和

3. 你真的要搬出去吗？你得想好。你_____搬出去，再想搬回来就不容易了。

    A. 反正   B. 千万   C. 回头   D. 一旦

4. 我刚才只是开玩笑，你_____别生气，我向你承认错误，好了吧。

    A. 回头   B. 一旦   C. 千万   D. 不在乎

5. 你的行李怎么还没有准备好呢？你带的东西太多了！毛巾、牙膏、洗衣粉这些日用品，中国_____！你只要带些常穿的衣服就行了！

    A. 应急   B. 现成的   C. 这倒好   D. 有的是

6. 早上王经理打电话让小张去他的办公室的时候，小张真_____公司要炒了他。

    A. 以为   B. 误会   C. 千万   D. 决定

7. 很多公司为了_____有硕士、博士学位的技术人员，付给他们很多钱。

    A. 在乎   B. 竞标   C. 留住   D. 轮到

（二）选择题

Circle the answer that best reflects the meaning of the sentence

1. 我们公司净是博士、硕士的，就是天上掉馅儿饼也轮不到我这个学士头上啊。（　　）

    A. 就是我们公司有好的项目，也不会给我，因为我的学历比较低。

    B. 如果我们公司有好东西，一般都给博士和硕士。

    C. 我们公司喜欢博士和硕士。

    D. 我们公司有好的项目，但是从来都不给只有学士学历的人。

2. 别人家都是丈夫说了算，我们家颠了个儿，妻子说了算。（　　）

    A. 别人家都是丈夫听妻子的，可是在我们家，妻子听丈夫的。

    B. 别人家都是妻子听丈夫的，可是我们家完全不一样，丈夫听妻子的。

    C. 我们家跟很多人家不一样。

    D. 我们家的做法不如别人家的做法好。

3. 炒你？公司留你还怕留不住呢！（　　）

    A. 公司认为你是最好的技术人员。

    B. 公司与其想让你离开，不如让你在这儿工作。

    C. 公司想让你住在这里。

    D. 公司绝对不会让你走！相反，还担心你想离开公司呢！

4. 这件事你不说我倒给忘了。（   ）

    A. 如果你没说这件事，我反而把这件事忘了

    B. 如果你没说这件事，我就真的把这件事忘了

    C. 如果你没说这件事，我就不想说了

    D. 如果你没说这件事，我并没有把这件事忘了

5. 我们先拿你妈的礼物应急，回头再给她买个更好的。（   ）

    A. 我们先给他买礼物，等一下再给你妈买礼物。

    B. 来不及给他买礼物了，我们只给你妈买一个好礼物吧。

    C. 我们给你妈买礼物买得太急，买错了。

    D. 现在来不及给他买礼物了，我们先把你妈的礼物送给他，然后再给你妈买一个更好的礼物。

6. 公司正在裁员，我这不是自己往枪口上撞吗？（   ）

    A. 公司正在裁员，我做这样的事，他们肯定不让我用枪。

    B. 公司正在裁员，我做这样的事，他们当然会让我死。

    C. 公司正在裁员，我做这样的事，他们也许会让我走。

    D. 公司正在裁员，我做这样的事，绝对是自己给自己找麻烦。

（三）选择适当的词语，替换句中的画线部分

Choose the most appropriate words to replace the underlined parts

A. 以为	B. 不在乎	C. 要是……的话	D. 往枪口上撞
E. 误会	F. 天上掉馅儿饼	G. 千万	H. 有的是
I. 回头	J. 一旦		

1. A：你最好别从网上下载音乐，<u>万一</u>查出来，你会被罚钱的。

    B：我<u>不怕</u>，再说，很多人都这样做。

    A：你别<u>认为</u>很多人都做的事情就不会出问题。

2. A：听说公司的王经理跟小张是一个大学毕业的，所以他把这个设计项目给小张了。

    B：可是，<u>如果</u>小张工作表现不好，王经理也不会给他。我相信，没有<u>不用努力就可以得到的好事</u>。

3. 喂，你是小王吗？我现在正在上班，<u>等一下</u>我给你打回去。

4. 李梅，请你<u>一定别想错了</u>，这张纸条是我给我女朋友写的，可是我把它放错了信箱了。

5. 现在的医学发展这么快，得了癌症以后被治好的人<u>很多</u>。

6. 他弟弟刚把他的新车撞了，你现在找他借车，这不是自己<u>找上门让他骂</u>吗！

（四）用所给词语完成对话

Complete the following dialogues with the items provided in the parenthesis

1. （回头，……的话）

A：对不起，我现在得去上课了，_____再给你打电话吧！

B：没关系，要是你忙_____，我们下个星期再说！

2. （天上掉馅儿饼，以为）

A：今天的考试我没有考好，哪儿有心情跟你去看电影啊！

B：那你昨天晚上干吗还去跳舞呢？我让你回宿舍你都不回！

A：我_____考试很容易呢。

B：就是容易，你也得学习呀！不学习，还想考得好，哪有_____的事啊！

3. （自己往枪口上撞，一旦）

A：如果你觉得你的老板做得不合适，你应该去找他的老板谈。

B：我可不去。_____我的老板知道了，那不是_____吗！？

4. （不在乎，误会，千万）

男朋友：昨天在图书馆跟你坐在一起的那个男生是谁？

女朋友：哦，是我的中国同学。我们俩人要一起做期末的中文对话。你_____别_____。

男朋友：我_____！

（五）角色扮演 Role play

Make a dialogue with a classmate. One party plays Xiao Zhang, and the other plays Director Wang. Your dialogue should incorporate the provided items.

小张	王经理
After you get the message that Director Wang is going to see you in his office, you know what will happen, and you are preparing yourself for the worst. However, you have to explain everything to him. At least let him know that you are not being unreasonable.	You are going to tell this young man, who is smart and promising, the decision about sending him to Shenzhen to do some further study so that he can get a promotion when he comes back.

1. 送礼	1. 从下星期开始，……
2. 千万	2. 忘了
3. 别误会	3. 拿回去
4. 炒我	4. 怕留不住

■ 三、课堂讨论 Discussion

1. 你认为小张是一个什么样的人？

2. 他的妻子李梅是一个什么样的人？

3. 你认为在中国送礼重要不重要？

4. 送礼这样的事情在你们国家也常常发生吗？

第十五课 倾 听

Please Listen More Carefully

编剧：彦坤

人物 （Characters）

爸爸 （bàba）——五十多岁。

晓玲 （Xiǎolíng）——二十五岁，女儿，文科大学毕业生。

陈娟 （Chén Juān）——女，二十六岁，文科大学毕业生。

面试领导 （miànshì lǐngdǎo）——男，四十岁。

课 文 Text

晓　玲：您知道那个**大名鼎鼎**[N1]的**黎明公司**吧，他现在**大客户部**正

1. 倾听	qīngtīng	v.	heed；listen attentively to
2. 文科	wénkē	n.	liberal arts；humanities
3. 毕业生	bìyèshēng	n.	graduate (of a school)
4. 面试	miànshì	v./n.	interview
5. 大名鼎鼎	dàmíng dǐngdǐng		famous；well-known；celebrated
6. 黎明公司	Límíng Gōngsī	N.	Daybreak Company(a company's name)
7. 客户	kèhù	n.	client；customer
8. 部	bù	n.	department (of a company)

对外招聘呢，而且名额**有限**。你姑娘我啊，就准备去应聘。

爸　爸：这可是大事啊，你得好好准备准备。

晓　玲：那还用说吗，我这叫**临阵磨枪**，不**快**也光[N2]。

爸　爸：晓玲……

晓　玲：爸，您听我说，您还**记**不记得我们班那陈娟——就是那个眼睛大大的那个**南京**姑娘……她呀，前几天也来北京了，好像也是为了这次招聘。

爸　爸：这么说[N3]陈娟是你的竞争**对手**了？

晓　玲：爸，您听我说，您现在知道她住哪ⅱ吗？

爸　爸：她住……

晓　玲：您甭猜了，我告诉您，她现在啊，和朋友租了一间**平房**，然后一天三**顿**饭全吃**方便面**，然后呢，就到图书馆呢去看书。您知道她都看什么书吗？

爸　爸：我也甭**瞎猜**了，还是你说吧。

9. 对外	duìwài		to the public
10. 招聘	zhāopìn	v.	hire; search (for a position)
11. 有限	yǒuxiàn	adj.	limited
12. 临阵磨枪	lín zhèn mó qiāng		(see note 2)
13. 快	kuài	adj.	(of a knife, spear, etc.) sharp
14. 记	jì	v.	remember
15. 南京	Nánjīng	N.	Nanjing (capital of Jiangsu Province)
16. 对手	duìshǒu	n.	opponent; adversary
17. 平房	píngfáng	n.	bungalow
18. 顿	dùn	m.	(a measure word for meals)
19. 方便面	fāngbiànmiàn	n.	instant noodles
20. 瞎猜	xiā cāi		guess blindly

晓　玲：她呀，借了一摞书，全都是关于礼仪方面的，什么[N4]怎么寒暄，怎么谈判，还有怎么握手书上都告诉她。你说这逗不逗?[N5]

爸　爸：这有什么好逗的? 握手本来……

晓　玲：爸，您听我说，人家呢，是大客户部，最重要的是信息。

爸　爸：晓玲……

晓　玲：爸，您听我跟您说，如今的商海呢，信息是命脉，掌握了信息就可以拯救一个企业……

爸　爸：人家聘用你不是让你去拯救人家的企业……

晓　玲：哎呀，爸，您别老打岔，我跟您说啊，我呢，都想好了，那天面试的时候，我打算大谈特谈一下我对于信息的把握，比如说，信息的重要性，那我想这样肯定能把考官

21.	摞	luò	m.	pile; stack
22.	关于	guānyú	prep.	about; pertaining to; concerning
23.	礼仪	lǐyí	n.	etiquette
24.	方面	fāngmiàn	n.	aspect; field
25.	寒暄	hánxuān	v.	exchange of pleasantries
26.	谈判	tánpàn	v.	talk, negotiate; talk, negotiation
27.	握手	wò shǒu	vo.	shake hands
28.	信息	xìnxī	n.	information
29.	如今	rújīn	t.	nowadays; now; today; at present
30.	商海	shānghǎi	n.	business world
31.	命脉	mìngmài	n.	lifeline
32.	拯救	zhěngjiù	v.	save; rescue
33.	企业	qǐyè	n.	enterprise; business; company
34.	聘用	pìnyòng	v.	hire; employ
35.	打岔	dǎ chà	vo.	interrupt (one's speech)
36.	大谈特谈	dà tán tè tán		speak (on a topic) extensively and heartily
37.	重要性	zhòngyàoxìng	n.	importance; significance
38.	考官	kǎoguān	n.	interviewer

紧紧地**握**在**手心**里。

爸　爸：我看**未必**，你看啊，你现在借了很多关于信息方面的书，我琢磨着，你应该像陈娟一样，多找一些**有关**礼仪方面的书。

晓　玲：……

爸　爸：晓玲，爸跟你说话呢。

晓　玲：爸，我听着呢！不就是关于礼仪吗，我跟您说啊，我从**幼儿园**开始就接受礼仪方面的教育，这对于我来说是**小儿科**[N6]。

39.	紧紧	jǐnjǐn		closely; tightly
40.	握	wò	v.	hold; grasp
41.	手心	shǒuxīn	n.	palm; control
42.	未必	wèibì	adv.	not necessarily
43.	有关	yǒuguān	v.	have something to do with
44.	幼儿园	yòu'éryuán	n.	kindergarten
45.	小儿科	xiǎo'érkē	n.	(see note 6)

爸　爸：你说的那些都是**基础**的礼仪，像你应聘这么大的公司，那**社交**礼仪也是非常重要的……

晓　玲：……

晓　玲：现在什么时代了，**信息时代**好不好[N7]，没信息没**知识**的，什么都甭谈，你看着我还笑。我说错了？你跟我说。

陈　娟：我这不是在听你说吗，你说得**兴致勃勃**[N8]的，我怎么**好意思打断**你啊。

晓　玲：哎，是我朋友，**比我爸强**，我爸他，甭跟他说，听不进去，一会儿就**不耐烦**了。

陈　娟：不会吧，我觉得**伯父**是一个很有**涵养**的人，**依我看**哪，没**准**儿是你话太**密**[N9]了。

46.	基础	jīchǔ	n.	foundation，basis
47.	社交	shèjiāo	n.	socializing
48.	信息时代	xìnxī shídài		IT age
49.	知识	zhīshi	n.	knowledge；know-how
50.	兴致勃勃	xìngzhì bóbó		full of zest or enthusiasm；in high spirits (also see note 8)
51.	好意思	hǎo yìsi		have the nerve (to do something improper)
52.	打断	dǎ duàn	vc.	interrupt (a speech，an action，etc.)
53.	比……强	bǐ……qiáng		better than…
54.	不耐烦	bú nàifán		impatient
55.	伯父	bófù	n.	uncle (a polite form of address for a man of one's father's generation)
56.	涵养	hányǎng	n.	self-restraint；virtue of patience；accomplishment in self-cultivation
57.	依我看	yī wǒ kàn		as I see it；in my opinion
58.	没准儿	méi zhǔnr	v.	不一定；perhaps；probably
59.	密	mì	adj.	dense；thick (also see note 9)

晓　玲：我话密？我就这脾气，改不了了。

陈　娟：晓玲啊，我们俩是**无话不谈**的好朋友吧，我觉得咱们在跟别人**交谈**时一定要眼里有事，心里有人[N10]，一定要**懂得尊重对方**，一句话，就是要学会倾听。

晓　玲：倾听？很重要吗？

爸　爸：当然重要了，这是对人最**起码**的尊重。

晓　玲：我知道错了，爸爸，刚才娟子已经**批评**过我了。我呀，以前总想，您就我这么一个宝贝女儿，又是在家，有什么礼仪可讲的，再说，您又不是不知道我，就这一**性格**。

爸　爸：讲**文明**礼仪可不分什么场合，当然，也不分什么性格，你说是不是啊？

晓　玲：嗯……

爸　爸：这还差不多。

60.	脾气	píqi	n.	temperament；disposition
61.	无话不谈	wú huà bù tán		keep no secret from each other
62.	交谈	jiāotán	v.	talk；converse
63.	懂得	dǒngde	v.	understand；know
64.	尊重	zūnzhòng	v.	respect
65.	对方	duìfāng	n.	the other person；the other side（in a conversation，negotiation，etc.）
66.	起码	qǐmǎ	adj.	the least；at least
67.	娟子	Juānzi	N.	(a nickname for Chen Juan)
68.	批评	pīpíng	v.	criticize
69.	性格	xìnggé	n.	personality
70.	文明	wénmíng	n.	civil，urbane；civilization

面试领导：现在我再问你最后一个问题，如果你被我们公司录用了，你将**面对**着很多的客户，在你和他们**接触**的**过程**当中，你**认为**哪些个语言能**表示**出对他们的尊重呢？

晓　　玲：一定要用语言表示是吗？

面试领导：是的。

晓　　玲：对不起，我**暂时**没有想好。

面试领导：**无非**[N11]是一些社交场合的**用语**，有那么难想吗？

晓　　玲：那倒也不是，只是依我个人**而言**[N12]，我认为，认真地倾听才是**尊敬**客户最好的表示方式。

71.	面对	miànduì	v.	face; confront
72.	接触	jiēchù	v.	contact
73.	过程	guòchéng	n.	course of events; process
74.	当中	dāngzhōng	n.	in the midst of; during
75.	认为	rènwéi	v.	consider; regard
76.	表示	biǎoshì	v.	express
77.	暂时	zànshí	adv.	for the time being; for the moment
78.	无非	wúfēi	adv.	nothing but; no more than (also see note 11)
79.	用语	yòngyǔ	n.	phraseology; term
80.	而言	ér yán		(used in the pattern 对……而言 duì...ér yán: in regard to...; also see note 12)
81.	尊敬	zūnjìng	v.	respect; honor

注释 **Notes**

1. **"大名鼎鼎"**:

    Being widely known; celebrated.

    成语，意思是：很有名。

    It is a set phrase often used to describe someone or some organization of broad renown.

    (1) 您知道那个大名鼎鼎的黎明公司吧，他现在大客户部正对外招聘呢。

    Do you know the famous Daybreak Company? Its Customer Service Department is now hiring.

    (2) 照片上的这个人就是大名鼎鼎的××先生。

    The man in the picture is none other than the preeminent Mr. so-and-so.

    (3) 听说那个大名鼎鼎的篮球教练，最近不当教练了。

    I heard that that celebrated basketball coach is not a coach any more.

2. **"临阵磨枪，不快也光"**:

    Last-minute preparation helps operation.

    意思是：快要打仗的时候磨枪，枪即使不快，也会很亮。常比喻考试或比赛前突击复习、准备，总会有一点儿效果。

    Literally, this popular saying means that to hone one's spear right before the battle at least makes the weapon brighter, if not really sharper. Metaphorically it suggests that a last-moment spurt, such as an intense review right before the exam, can always make a difference.

3. **"这么说……"**:

    In that case...

    根据对方的话得出的推论。在句子中起连接的作用。后边常接一个疑问句。

    The phrase leads a conclusion based on the information provided by the other person. It thus functions as a joint in the dialogue, and is often followed by a question.

    (1) 晓玲：爸，您听我说，您还记不记得我们班那陈娟——就是那个眼睛大大的那个南京姑娘……她呀，前几天也来北京了，好像也是为了这次招聘。

Xiaoling：Listen，Dad. Do you remember my former classmate Chen Juan, that girl from Nanjing with big eyes？.... She also came to Beijing a few days ago，probably for the job interview as well.

爸爸：这么说陈娟是你的竞争对手了？

Father：In that case，wouldn't Chen Juan become an adversary for you？

(2) A：我今天要准备明天的考试，……

　　Today I have to prepare for tomorrow's test...

　　B：这么说，你不想去看晚上的演出了？太可惜了。

　　Does that mean you don't want to see the performance tonight？ What a shame!

(3) A：我从来没见过这个人。

　　I have never met that guy.

　　B：这么说，你不认识他？

　　So you actually don't know him？

4. "什么"：

用于列举。口语。

"什么"可以用在一些并列的成分前，表示随意列举。

In spoken Chinese，"什么" can be used to lead a juxtaposition of multiple items.

(1) 她呀，借了一摞书，全都是关于礼仪方面的，什么怎么寒暄，怎么谈判，还有怎么握手书上都告诉她。

She borrowed a whole bunch of books, all about different aspects of etiquette such as how to exchange greetings and how to handle a negotiation. The books even teach how to shake hands.

(2) 他上街买了好多东西。什么衣服、文具、日用品……满满一车。

He went shopping and bought many things, such as clothes, stationery, and daily necessities... A full carload of them.

(3) 我喜欢的运动很多，什么打篮球，打乒乓球，游泳，跑步，我都喜欢。

I like many sports. Basketball, ping-pong, swimming, running—I like them all.

列举比较正式的项目、严肃的事项时，前面不宜用"什么"。

For a juxtaposition of multiple items in a formal writing，however，"什么" should not be used.

5. **"你说这逗不逗"**：

Isn't it funny?

"逗" 在这里的意思是 "可笑"。口语。

"逗" is a colloquialism that means "laughable" or "amusing".

6. **"这对我来说是小儿科"**：

It is something most rudimentary to me.

"小儿科" 本来是指医院里给小孩子看病的那一科，经常用来比喻自己认为比较容易的事情。口语。

In its original sense，"小儿科" means pediatrics，but as a colloquialism it refers metaphorically to things one considers simple and easy.

(1) 不就是关于礼仪吗，我跟您说啊，我从幼儿园开始就接受礼仪方面的教育，这对于我来说是小儿科。

Isn't it just etiquette? Let me tell you, I have learned etiquette ever since I was in the kindergarten. It's no big deal for me.

(2) 买房子贷款？不难，对我来说那是小儿科。

To get a mortgage loan to buy a house? No problem，it's just a piece of cake for me.

7. **"现在什么时代了，信息时代好不好"**：

What age is it now? Isn't it the IT age?

这句话的意思是：你应该知道，现在是信息时代了。口语。

The question "信息时代好不好" is a colloquial way to say：You should be aware that it is now the IT age.

8. **"兴致勃勃"**：

成语，形容兴趣很浓、情绪很高的样子。

This set phrase describes a person who is enthusiastic and in high spirits.

(1) 你说得兴致勃勃的，我怎么好意思打断你啊。

You were speaking so enthusiastically, and how could I bear to interrupt you?

(2) 我进去的时候，看见他正在兴致勃勃地给大家介绍这次会议的情况。

When I entered, I saw him zestfully briefing everyone about the conference.

(3) 穿好衣服，他们就兴致勃勃地参加舞会去了。

　　Having dressed up, they went to the dancing party cheerfully.

9. **"话太密"**:

　　意思是：说话一句接一句，中间较少停顿。

　　Literally, "话太密" means "the words are too dense". In the play, it means there are few pauses in the flow of words, which makes it difficult for someone else to chip in.

晓玲：是我朋友，比我爸强，我爸他，甭跟他说，听不进去，一会儿就不
　　　耐烦了。

Xiaoling：You're my true friend, better than my dad. I just can't talk to him. He simply wouldn't listen, and would get impatient momentarily.

陈娟：不会吧，我觉得伯父是一个很有涵养的人，依我看哪，没准儿是你
　　　话太密了。

Chen Juan：How could that be? I think your dad is man of remarkable self-restraint. As I see it, it was probably because you spoke in that rolling way.

10. **"跟别人交谈时一定要眼里有事，心里有人"**:

　　这句话的意思是：跟别人谈话时，眼睛要注意周围的事情，心里要想着对方。

　　Literally, this sentence means：When you talk to someone, you must have things in your eyes and the person in your mind. What is suggested is：During a conversation, one should be observant of the ambient circumstances and be thoughtful about the other person.

11. **"无非"**:

　　意思是：只（不过）。多出现于正式的口语。

　　The term "无非" is roughly an equivalent to "只"（only）or "不过"（no more than）. It is often used on more formal occasions.

(1) 面试领导：你认为哪些个语言能表示出对他们的尊重呢？

　　Interviewer：What words do you think can express your respect for them?

　　……

　　晓玲：对不起，我暂时没有想好。

　　Xiaoling：Sorry, I haven't thought it well for the moment.

面试领导：无非是一些社交场合的用语，有那么难想吗？

Interviewer：Just some socializing formulas. Do you have to think that hard?

（2）我无非跟你开个玩笑，你干吗那么生气？

I was just kidding. Why were you so angry?

（3）我没买什么值钱的东西，无非是一些日用品。

I didn't buy anything expensive，only some daily necessities.

12. **"依我个人而言"：**

这句话的意思在这里是：按照我个人的看法。

In the context of the play, this structure means "in my personal view" or "from my personal perspective".

听说练习　Listening & Speaking Exercises

一、课文理解 Text Comprehension

(一) 根据故事情节选择适当的答案

Please choose the most appropriate answer based on the story

1. 晓玲现在在找（　　　）
   A. 竞争对手　　　　　　B. 陈娟　　　　　　　C. 工作

2. 黎明公司怎么样？（　　　）
   A. 兴致勃勃　　　　　　B. 临阵磨枪　　　　　C. 大名鼎鼎

3. 陈娟在看哪方面的书？（　　　）
   A. 小儿科　　　　　　　B. 礼仪　　　　　　　C. 信息

4. 晓玲认为面试的时候哪方面的知识最重要？（　　　）
   A. 礼仪　　　　　　　　B. 信息　　　　　　　C. 教育

5. 晓玲的爸爸认为面试的时候哪方面的知识最重要？（　　　）
   A. 倾听　　　　　　　　B. 信息　　　　　　　C. 礼仪

6. 晓玲以为自己比陈娟（　　　）
   A. 学习更好　　　　　　B. 书看得多　　　　　C. 知道得多

7. 陈娟觉得谁是一个很有涵养的人？（　　　）
   A. 她伯父　　　　　　　B. 晓玲的伯父　　　　C. 晓玲的爸爸

8. 晓玲面试的时候说什么是尊敬客户最好的表示方式？（　　　）
   A. 懂社交礼仪　　　B. 兴致勃勃地说话　　C. 认真地倾听

(二) 根据课文判断下面句子意思的正误

State whether the following statements are true or false based on the story

1. （　　　）黎明公司是一家很有名的大公司。

2. （　　　）黎明公司的大客户部要招聘很多人。

3. （　　　）晓玲和陈娟是非常好的朋友。

4.（　　）晓玲认为陈娟看的那些关于礼仪方面的书对找工作没用。

5.（　　）晓玲认为礼仪对于她来说是小菜一碟。

6.（　　）晓玲的爸爸认为讲文明礼仪不分场合，也不分性格。

7.（　　）晓玲认为面试的时候一个人对于信息的把握能给考官留下很深的印象。

8.（　　）晓玲的爸爸建议晓玲应该像陈娟一样，多找一些有关礼仪方面的书看看。

（三）先听故事叙述，然后复述故事
Listen to the narrative first and then retell the story

晓玲告诉爸爸，大名鼎鼎的黎明公司大客户部正在对外招聘，她准备去应聘。在晓玲看来，如今的商海，信息是命脉，掌握了信息就可以拯救一个企业，所以她打算面试的时候，大谈特谈信息的重要以及她对于信息的把握，她认为这样肯定能把考官紧紧握在她的手心里。

晓玲的同学陈娟也要去应聘。她认为陈娟从图书馆借的全都是关于礼仪方面的书，很可笑。可是爸爸不同意她的看法，建议她也应该多学习礼仪方面的知识，她却说她上幼儿园的时候就已经接受礼仪教育了。

陈娟是一个善于听取别人意见的人，晓玲跟她谈话以后，觉得陈娟说的"一定要学会懂得尊重对方，要学会倾听别人的意见"是对的。在面试的时候，她对最后一个问题的回答就是："我认为，认真地倾听才是尊敬客户最好的表示方式。"要是晓玲最后得到了这份工作，她应该感谢陈娟和爸爸。

■ 二、词语使用 Application of Vocabulary and Grammar

（一）选择题
Choose the item that is grammatically correct

1. 陈娟前几天也从南京来北京了，好像也是＿＿＿＿＿＿这次招聘。

　　A. 为了　　　　　B. 面谈　　　　　C. 由于　　　　　D. 因为

2. 陈娟现在和朋友租了一间平房，一天三顿饭全吃方便面，＿＿＿＿＿＿呢，就到图书馆呢去看书。

　　A. 然后　　　　　B. 今后　　　　　C. 以后　　　　　D. 后来

3. 您知道她＿＿＿＿＿＿看什么书吗？

　　A. 还　　　　　　B. 才　　　　　　C. 都　　　　　　D. 就

4. 我也甭瞎猜了，＿＿＿＿＿＿你说吧。

A. 就是   B. 反正   C. 而且   D. 还是

5. 她看的书都是关于礼仪方面的，_____怎么寒暄，怎么谈判，还有怎么握手……，你说这逗不逗？

    A. 哪儿   B. 跟谁   C. 什么   D. 礼仪

6. 爸爸，您听我_____您说，如今的商海，信息是命脉，掌握了信息就可以拯救一个企业。

    A. 替   B. 向   C. 跟   D. 给

7. 爸，我听_____呢！不就是关于礼仪吗，我都懂！

    A. 了   B. 过   C. 着   D. 听

8. 晓玲啊，我们俩是_____的好朋友吧，我觉得咱们在跟别人交谈时一定要多听听别人有什么想法。

    A. 兴致勃勃   B. 大谈特谈   C. 大名鼎鼎   D. 无话不谈

(二) 选择题

Circle the answer that best reflects the meaning of the underlined portion of the sentence

1. 黎明公司现在正对外招聘呢。你<u>姑娘</u>我啊，就准备去应聘。（　　）

    A. 女儿

    B. 姑姑

    C. 小姐

    D. 阿姨

2. 我觉得伯父是一个很有涵养的人，依我看哪，<u>没准儿</u>是你的话没道理。（　　）

    A. 没准备

    B. 一定

    C. 不一定

    D. 也许

3. 你是我朋友，比我爸强，我说话，我爸<u>听不进去</u>，一会儿就不耐烦了。（　　）

    A. 听不懂

    B. 听不清楚

    C. 不想听

    D. 听不见

4. 掌握信息考官就聘你了？我看未必。（　　）

    A. 不一定

    B. 一定

    C. 必须

    D. 未来

5. 那天面试的时候，我打算大谈特谈一下我对于信息的把握。（　　）

    A. 好好谈谈

    B. 大声地谈

    C. 无话不谈

    D. 谈大事情

（三）选择适当的词语，替换句中的画线部分

Choose the most appropriate words to replace the underlined parts

> A. 小儿科　B. 大名鼎鼎　C. 什么　D. 这对你来说……　E. 无非

1. 娟子不过就批评了你两句，有什么好生气的？

2. 照片上的这个人就是非常有名的××先生。

3. 开学了，他买了好多东西。像冰箱、电视机、沙发等等满满一车。

4. 少花钱多办事，你做起来是很难的，可对于我小菜一碟，不就一只箱子吗？

5. 修个电脑，拉根电线，这种事对他来说太简单了。

（四）用所给词语完成对话

Complete the following dialogues with the items provided in the parenthesis

1.（这么说，什么……）

    A：不知道北京的工作好不好找。

    B：现在大名鼎鼎的公司，像_____黎明公司、长城公司、太平洋公司，都在对外招聘人呢。

    A：_____，我找工作还是有希望的了。

2.（我看未必……；临阵磨枪，不快也光）

    A：今晚不能陪你，我要准备明天的考试。

    B：平时不用功，今晚就是一夜不睡觉，_____你就能考得很好。

    A：_____，你没听说过吗？

3.（你别老打岔，有涵养，这么说）

    晓玲：爸，您还记得我们班那个叫陈娟的南京姑娘吧？她也去应聘。

爸爸：记得，一个很_____的姑娘。_____陈娟是你的竞争
    对手了？

晓玲：爸，您听我说，她现在和朋友租了一间平房，一天三顿饭全吃
    方便面……

爸爸：你什么意思？

晓玲：然后呢，就到图书馆去看书。您知道……

爸爸：看书有什么不好？

晓玲：_____，听我说完你再说，好不好？

4.（最起码，无非）

爸爸：晓玲常说别人不好，_____是认为自己各个方面的条件
    都好。

陈娟：我也觉得她有时不爱听别人的意见，好像她认为别人都该听
    她的。

爸爸：这样很不好。学会倾听是非常重要的，这是对人_____的
    尊重。

（五）角色扮演 Role play

Make a dialogue with a classmate. One party plays Xiaoling, and the other
plays Her father. Your dialogue should incorporate the provided items.

晓玲	爸爸
You are telling your father that a celebrated company is hiring and you are preparing yourself for an interview. You think your friend, Xiaojuan, is naïve for reading a lot of books on social etiquette in preparation for the same interview, since in your opinion, nowadays, one's knowledge on what's going on in the market place is crucial for getting the job because information is the lifeline of the business world.	You tell your daughter her interview is important for getting the job. She must prepare herself well. You are skeptical of your daughter's criticism of Xiaojuan for believing that one's knowledge of social etiquette is important.

1. 大名鼎鼎　　2. 名额有限 3. 应聘 4. 临阵磨枪，不快也光 5. 一天三顿　　6. 关于礼仪方面 7. 信息　　　　8. 商海 9. 命脉　　　　10. 别老打岔 11. 紧握在手心里 12. 接受……的教育 13. 小儿科	1. 大事 2. 好好准备 3. 竞争对手 4. 瞎猜 5. 我琢磨着 6. 基础的礼仪 7. 社交礼仪

三、课堂讨论 Discussion

1. 你对晓玲这个人有什么看法？你喜欢跟她这样的人交朋友吗？为什么？

2. 在你看来，一个在客户部工作的人哪些条件比较重要？

3. 要是你是考官，你需要在晓玲和陈娟两人之中选一个，你会选谁？为什么？

第十六课 退 书

Returning a Book

编剧：曾有情

人物 (Characters)

亚平 （Yàpíng） —— 男，二十多岁，安琪的丈夫。

安琪 （Ān Qí） —— 女，二十多岁。

营业员 （yíngyèyuán） —— 女，二十多岁。

课 文 Text

安　琪：哎哟喂，亚平，我刚把书柜整理好，你怎么搞得乱七八糟的。

亚　平：哎呀，"书到用时方恨少[N1]啊" ——这东西也跟钱似的。

安　琪：行了，行了，你说吧，你找什么书啊？

---

1. 退	tuì	v.	return
2. 丈夫	zhàngfu	n.	husband
3. 营业员	yíngyèyuán	n.	store clerk; shop assistant
4. 书柜	shūguì	n.	bookcase
5. 乱七八糟	luàn qi bā zāo	adj.	in a mess; mess-up

亚　平：写一篇短文，要引用《史记》里面的两个典故。

安　琪：我跟你说啊，咱家没这本书，甭瞎折腾^{N2}了，啊！

亚　平：不是，别的书里也有，找不着了。

安　琪：你买一本《史记》不得了嘛^{N3}。

亚　平：哎哟，我的姑奶奶，这短文发表得了发表不了还是回事呢^{N4}，就是让编辑部发表了，压成豆腐块^{N5}，也就几十块钱稿费；可是你买一本《史记故事》就上百^{N6}，一点儿经济头脑都没有！

安　琪：买吧你又舍不得，找又找不着，那怎么办？你总不能把书店搬回家吧！

亚　平：书店？……

营业员：你好。

安　琪：哦，请问有《史记故事》吗？

6. 短文	duǎnwén	n.	short article; essay
7. 引用	yǐnyòng	v.	quote; cite
8. 史记	Shǐjì	N.	Records of the Historian(book name)
9. 典故	diǎngù	n.	allusion; literary quotation
10. 折腾	zhēteng	v.	do sth. over and over again; turn from side to side
11. 发表	fābiǎo	v.	publish (articles, etc.)
12. 编辑部	biānjíbù	n.	editorial department
13. 压成	yā chéng	vc.	(see note 5)
14. 豆腐块	dòufukuài	n.	(see note 5)
15. 稿费	gǎofèi	n.	author's remuneration
16. 上百	shàng bǎi		reach one hundred
17. 头脑	tóunǎo	n.	brains; mind
18. 舍不得	shěbude	v.	relunctant to (spend money)

营业员：哦，有，您跟我来。

营业员：昨天还在这儿呢，怎么没了？

营业员：谁搁这儿了，给您。

安　琪：谢谢。

安　琪：算是我给你的礼物。

亚　平：哎，这谁叫你买的？

安　琪：人家^{N7}是想给你个惊喜。

亚　平：哎呀，我这**文章**都写完了，你还买书干什么呀？

安　琪：啊？

安　琪：哎，小姐，我昨天在这儿买了一套书，请问能退吗？

营业员：您买的是什么书啊？

安　琪：《史记故事》。

营业员：噢，我**记起来**了，昨天是您在这儿买的那本书，我们**正要**
　　　　找您呢，您看这——

19. 文章	wénzhāng	n.	article; essay
20. 记起来	jì qilai	vc.	remember; recall
21. 正要	zhèng yào		be just about to

启　事

6月25日在本店^{N8}购买《史记故事》的顾客请注意，由于该书^{N9}有**缺页**，请您见到启事后，尽快与我们**联系**。

安　琪：哟，这套书是**残书**啊，那我就更不能买了。

营业员：哦，没关系，您先别着急，我们可以给您退！

安　琪：那太好了。可是今天我是**顺路**问问，书没带来。

营业员：没关系，您**改天**带来就可以了。

安　琪：可我明天就要**出差**了，好几天才能回来呢。

营业员：那要不这样，我跟您去**取**一下吧。

安　琪：那合适吗？

营业员：没关系，因为我们一直在找这套书，今天**终于**^{N10}找到了。

安　琪：快请进，请进，坐。

营业员：谢谢。

22.	启事	qǐshì	n.	notice; announcement
23.	购买	gòumǎi	v.	buy; purchase
24.	顾客	gùkè	n.	customer; shopper
25.	由于	yóuyú	prep.	as a result of; due to
26.	缺页	quē yè	vo.	missing page
27.	联系	liánxì	v.	contact; get in touch with
28.	残书	cán shū		damaged book
29.	顺路	shùnlù	adv.	in passing; while on the way
30.	改天	gǎitiān	adv.	another day; some other day
31.	出差	chū chāi	vo.	be away on a business trip
32.	取	qǔ	v.	take; get; fetch
33.	终于	zhōngyú	adv.	at last; in the end; finally

安　琪：亚平，把昨天咱们买的那套《史记故事》拿出来。

亚　平：咳，拿……拿它干什么？

营业员：那套《史记故事》里有缺页。

亚　平：啊？不会吧？

营业员：书店里有一个不文明的**读者**，他**偷偷**把自己**需要**的书**页撕**下来**带走**了，我们经理也是昨天**偶然**发现这套书里有缺页，就把它收了起来。我不知道这件事情，又把书卖给了这位大姐。

安　琪：你说这人多**缺德**，啊，你把书撕了，人还怎么卖呀，是不是？

亚　平：是，是……

安　琪：哎，对了，你呀，**专门**写篇文章给他**曝**曝**光**，让他**丢人现眼**[N11]！

亚　平：对，对……

安　琪：你看人家多热情，我到书店看见一**告示**，让咱们去退书，你看人家来取书来了。

34.	读者	dúzhě	n.	reader
35.	偷偷	tōutōu	adv.	stealthily; secretly
36.	需要	xūyào	v. /n.	need; want
37.	页	yè	m.	page
38.	撕	sī	v.	tear; rip
39.	带走	dài zǒu	vc.	take away
40.	偶然	ǒurán	adv. /adj.	accidentally
41.	缺德	quē dé	vo.	have no regard for other members of society; wicked
42.	专门	zhuānmén	adv.	especially (for a certain purpose)
43.	曝光	bào guāng	vo.	expose (wrong doing in the newspaper or on TV)
44.	丢人现眼	diū rén xiàn yǎn		lose face; be embarrassed
45.	告示	gàoshi	n.	official notice

营业员：我们做**生意**呀，其实就是讲究一个**诚信**，我们不能把自己
　　　　的损失**转嫁**给顾客呀。

亚　平：是，是……

安　琪：你们想得真够**周到**的。

营业员：哎，那你们把书给我，我把书**款**退给你们。

安　琪：好。

亚　平：哦，不，不……

亚　平：书我们就不退了……

安　琪：亚平，你昨天还让我把书**退回去**呢，今儿怎么不退了？

亚　平：是……我又想要那套书了。

营业员：那我回去**请示**一下我们经理，给你们**打个折**，你们看好
　　　　不好？

亚　平：哦，不，不……不用了。

营业员：那等你们商量好了，可以**随时**去找我，那我先走了，
　　　　再见。

亚　平：**慢走**。

安　琪：谢谢啊！

46. 生意	shēngyi	n.	business
47. 诚信	chéngxìn	n.	sincerity and honesty
48. 转嫁	zhuǎnjià	v.	pass (the responsibility, blame, etc.) to someone else
49. 周到	zhōudào	adj.	thoughtful; considerate
50. 款	kuǎn	n.	money; cash
51. 退回去	tuì huiqu	vc.	return
52. 请示	qǐngshì	v.	ask for or request instructions
53. 打(个)折	dǎ (ge) zhé	vo.	allow a discount
54. 随时	suíshí	adv.	at any time; at all times
55. 慢走	màn zǒu		take care

安　琪：你怎么回事啊，一会_儿这样一会_儿**那样**的[N12]？人家上门服
　　　　务，你最起码的**礼貌**都没有……

亚　平：不是，他是这么回事——那书，它是我撕的！

安　琪：你……

56.	那样	nàyàng	pron.	that way; like that
57.	上门	shàngmén	v.	drop in; visit
58.	礼貌	lǐmào	n.	courtesy; politeness

注释 Notes

1. **"书到用时方恨少"**:

这是一句俗语。"方"的意思是"才"。这个俗语是说，到用到某种知识的时候，才悔恨自己读的书太少了。这句话常用来感叹自己读的书少，也可以用来劝别人多读书。

"Only at the time when one needs knowledge does one realize that he has not learned enough." This idiom says that you would regret you didn't learn enough only when you need a certain knowledge. One can also use this sentence to advise young people to never stop learning.

2. **"折腾"**:

意思是反复做某个动作。本课中的句子是："我跟你说啊，咱家没这本书，甭瞎折腾了，啊！"这里指到处翻书、找书。

"折腾" refers to doing something repeatedly, for example, in this story: "I tell you, we don't have the book, quit searching for it and making a mess of everything!"

3. **"你买一本《史记》不得了嘛"**:

这是一个反问句，意思是"你买一本《史记》得了"。"得了"用在陈述句的末尾，可以表示肯定，可以加强语气，对整个句子不增加新的意思。

"Why don't you simply buy a copy of《史记》?" This is a rhetorical question, indicating that it is the easiest thing to just go buy the book (instead of searching for it at home). "得了" attached to the end of an affirmative sentence, only functions to strengthen the assertion. See more examples below.

(1) 明天的会你去得了，我有事，去不了。

Why don't you go to the meeting tomorrow? I'm busy and won't make it.

(2) 买辆新车得了，旧车老出毛病。

Go get a new car. This old one has many problems.

(3) 咱们去英国得了，日本太贵。

Let's go to England instead. Life in Japan is too expensive.

4. **"这篇短文发表得了发表不了还是回事呢"**:

"还是回事呢" 意思是：还是一个问题呢。整个句子的意思是：这篇短文还不一定能不能发表呢。

"还是回事呢" means "is another matter". The whole sentence "这篇短文发表得了发表不了还是回事呢" (Whether the article will be published or not is a different matter) indicates that the speaker is not sure of the publication of his article.

5. **"压成豆腐块"**:

"压" 是 "压缩" 的意思。"豆腐块" 常用来比喻报纸上发表的篇幅很短的文章。"压成豆腐块" 的意思是：把文章压缩得很短。

"压" is "压缩" (condense). "豆腐块" a piece of dried tofu. It is often used to refer to short articles on the newspaper (that literally occupies the size of a piece of dried tofu).

6. **"上百"**:

"上百" 的意思是：用 "百" 来计算。本课的句子："可是你买一本《史记故事》就上百，一点儿经济头脑都没有!" 意思是一本《史记故事》要一百来（多）块钱，……。

"上百" means "reaching the figure of one hundred". "If you buy a copy of《史记故事》, that would cost you about/over a hundred. You have no sense of math!"

7. **"人家"**:

代词 "人家" 可以代别人，也可以代说话人自己（女孩子喜欢用）。口语。

"人家", a pronoun, normally refers to other people. However, it can be used to refer to oneself, usually by young women in colloquial speech.

(1) 亚平：哎，这谁叫你买的？

Yaping：Hey, who told you to buy that?

安琪：人家是想给你个惊喜。

Anqi：Somebody (I) was trying to surprise you.

(2) 你给我买吧，人家喜欢嘛!

Please buy it for me, I really like it.

(3) 人家头疼，你还叫我给你做饭。

I have a headache, yet you still want me to cook for you.

8. **"本店"**:

　　"本人"指说话人自己；"本"用在集体、机构等前表示说话人所在的集体、机构等。书面语。下面是本课书店启事中的句子：

　　　　6月25日在本店购买《史记故事》的顾客请注意，……

　　"本人" refers to the speaker. "本" can be also used before an organization and institution to represent the speaker's affiliation. It is often seen in a formal writing. Here is an example from this lesson：

　　　　Attention please，

　　　　Those who purchased《史记故事》in this store on June 25th...

　　这里"本店"就是登启事的书店。

　　Here "本店" refers to the book store which posted this announcement.

　　还可以说"本校""本班""本系""本院""本公司"等等。

　　We can also say "本校"、"本班"、"本系"、"本院"、"本公司" etc.

9. **"该书"**:

　　"该"可以作指示代词，指代上面刚刚提到过的人或事物，作用同"那"，后面不用量词。多用于书面。

　　"该" can be used as a demonstrative，referring to a person or an entity mentioned earlier. This function of "该" is the same as "那"，but it is not followed by a measure word，and it is used in more formal writing.

10. **"终于"**:

　　　　at last，finally

　　　　表示经过较长过程最后出现了某种结果。多用于希望的结果。

　　After a long process，eventually the desired outcome takes place.

　　（1）因为我们一直在找这套书，今天终于找到了……

　　　　We had been searching for this set of books all the time，and finally found it today.

　　（2）上了四年大学，今天终于毕业了。

　　　　Finally we are graduating today after four years in college.

　　（3）这两个好朋友分别很长时间了，今天终于见面了，所以特别高兴。

　　　　These two good friends，after being parted for a long time，finally saw each other today，and were so thrilled.

11. **"丢人现眼"**:

　　　　lose face

　　　　"丢人"和"现眼"的意思都是"丧失体面"。也可以说"丢脸""丢面子"。口语。

　　"丢人" and "现眼" both mean "to lose face". One can also say "丢脸"、"丢面子".

12. **"一会_儿这样一会_儿那样的"：**

　　意思是"多变"（erratic）。

（1）你怎么回事啊，一会_儿这样一会_儿那样的？

What's the matter with you? You've been changing all the time.

（2）你刚才说去，现在又说不去。你怎么一会_儿这样一会_儿那样的？

A moment ago you said you would go and now you are saying you won't. Why this flip-flop?

（3）他这个人多变，一会_儿这样，一会_儿那样，你不知道他到底想怎么样。

He changes all the time. You never know what he is thinking.

听说练习 Listening & Speaking Exercises

■ 一、课文理解 Text Comprehension

（一）根据故事情节选择适当的答案

Please choose the most appropriate answer based on the story

1. 亚平找书是为了（   ）

　　A. 整理书柜

　　B. 找两个《史记》中的典故

　　C. 学习《史记》

2. 亚平不想买《史记》这套书，因为他觉得（   ）

　　A. 他的文章不一定能发表

　　B. 买一套《史记故事》很贵，文章的稿费太少

　　C. 上边两个回答都对

3. 安琪买《史记故事》是为了（   ）

　　A. 给亚平一个惊喜

　　B. 自己想看这套书

　　C. 亚平可以拿很多稿费

4. 安琪不知道亚平已经去书店（   ）

　　A. 把《史记故事》买回家来了

　　B. 把《史记故事》退了

　　C. 把《史记故事》里边他需要的书页撕下来带走了

5. 缺页是（   ）

　　A. 读者发现的

　　B. 是营业员发现的

　　C. 是经理发现的

6. 营业员来到亚平和安琪家（   ）

　　A. 来取书退钱

B. 来问亚平撕书页的事

　　C. 来找缺页

7. 亚平不愿意退书，因为他（　　　）

　　A. 不想让别人知道是他撕的书页

　　B. 觉得自己错了

　　C. 确实想买这套书

8. 这个书店的经理认为，要想做好生意（　　　）

　　A. 顾客最重要　　　　B. 卖的书不缺页最重要　　　C. 信誉最重要

（二）根据课文判断下面句子意思的正误

State whether the following statements are true or false based on the story

1. （　　）亚平以前有一本《史记》，可是找不到了。

2. （　　）安琪花钱比较仔细。

3. （　　）安琪比亚平舍得花钱。

4. （　　）安琪明天可以来书店退书。

5. （　　）安琪买了缺页的书，营业员觉得对不起她。

6. （　　）亚平不愿意退书，因为这是他做的错事。

7. （　　）亚平跟营业员认错了。

（三）先听故事叙述，然后复述故事

Listen to the narrative first and then retell the story

　　亚平的文章就要写完了，但是他需要看一下《史记故事》里的两个典故。亚平的妻子安琪想给丈夫一个惊喜，下班以后去书店买了一套《史记故事》。可是，回家以后才知道，丈夫已经把文章写完不需要看那本书了。

　　第二天，安琪去书店问能不能退《史记故事》，营业员告诉她这套书里有缺页，他们正在找买书的人，要退顾客钱呢。可是安琪带营业员回家来拿书的时候，亚平反而一定要留下这本有缺页的书。安琪觉得很奇怪，营业员走了以后，亚平才告诉安琪，原来书里的缺页是他撕的。现在他买了这套书就是为了以后不再做这样的错事了。

■　二、词语使用 Application of Vocabulary and Grammar

（一）选择题

Choose the item that is grammatically correct

1. 这篇文章，我已经写了两个星期了，今天_____写完了！

　　A. 随时　　　B. 惊喜　　　C. 终于　　　D. 起码

2. 这是我的手机号，你要是有问题_____给我打电话。

　　A. 顺路　　　　B. 随时　　　　C. 偶然　　　　D. 改天

3. 别再想昨天的考试了，你下次努力考好一点儿_____。

　　A. 终于　　　　B. 惊喜　　　　C. 一百分　　　D. 不得了嘛

4. 哪些技术人员能参加竞标得先_____公司老板才能决定。

　　A. 请示　　　　B. 讲究　　　　C. 商量　　　　D. 算是

5. 这不是你爸爸刚给你买的新电脑吗？我用_____吗？

　　A. 丢人　　　　B. 舍不得　　　C. 礼貌　　　　D. 合适

6. 今年他买了一辆新车，可是_____开。出去玩儿的时候，总坐别人的车。

　　A. 随时　　　　B. 顺路　　　　C. 偶然　　　　D. 舍不得

（二）选择题

Circle the answer that best reflects the meaning of the sentence

1. 你怎么一点儿经济头脑都没有！（　　　）

　　A. 你太舍不得花钱

　　B. 你应该学一点儿经济

　　C. 你完全不知道应该怎样省钱

　　D. 你花钱以前要跟我商量

2. 这篇短文发表得了发表不了还是一回事呢。（　　　）

　　A. 这篇短文能不能发表很重要

　　B. 这篇短文可能会发表

　　C. 我不知道这篇短文能不能发表

　　D. 我得问一问才知道这篇短文能不能发表

3. 这篇短文就是让编辑部发表了，压成豆腐块，也就几十块钱稿费。

　　　　　　　　　　　　　　　　　　　　　　　　　（　　　）

　　A. 编辑部不会发表这篇文章，因为太短了

　　B. 我不会让编辑部发表这篇文章，因为稿费太少

　　C. 如果编辑部同意发表这篇文章，（这篇文章）也会很短，稿费也不多

　　D. 编辑部说要是他们发表这篇文章，可以给几十块钱

4. 做生意其实就讲究一个诚信。（　　　）

　　A. 做生意最重要的就是相信别人

B. 做生意最重要的就是让别人相信自己

C. 做生意最重要的就是对人说真话

D. 做生意最重要的就是相信别人，也相信自己

5. 我们不能把自己的损失转嫁给顾客。（　　）

A. 我们不能让顾客吃亏

B. 我们不能让自己吃亏

C. 我们自己吃了亏可以从顾客那里赚钱

D. 你不要嫁给顾客

6. 你应该写篇文章给他曝曝光，让他丢人现眼。（　　）

A. 你应该让他写一篇文章，他会觉得丢脸

B. 你写一篇文章，他会觉得丢脸

C. 你应该写一篇文章让他看，他会觉得丢脸

D. 你应该写一篇文章让别人都知道这件事，让他丢脸

7. 你怎么回事啊，一会儿这样一会儿那样的？（　　）

A. 你等一会儿要回家吗？

B. 你为什么老改变你的想法？

C. 你到底一会儿要做什么？

D. 你一会儿有什么事？

（三）选择适当的词语，替换句中的画线部分

Choose the most appropriate words to replace the underlined parts

A. 舍不得	B. 不得了嘛	C. 找不着	D. 随时
E. 乱七八糟	F. 终于	G. 丢人现眼	H. 偶然
I. 折腾	J. 舍不得	K. 不得了嘛	

1. 你要是不放心她，每天给她打个电话就行了。

2. 让圆圆的爸爸在那么多同学面前给圆圆道歉，那不是太丢面子吗！

3. 虽然他赚的钱不少，但是他还是不愿意花上百块钱买一双运动鞋。

4. 你要是有问题什么时候都可以来问我。

5. 秦悦今年春天去检查身体，没想到检查出了白血病。

6. 他一直想去中国学中文，但是因为钱不够，不能去。去年他每天去饭馆儿打工，最后，钱够了，今年夏天他就能去中国了！

7. A：你又在翻我的书架干什么？翻得这么乱？

B：我在给你整理书架呢！我看你的书太多了，给别人吧，你<u>不愿意</u>，可是找什么东西都找不到！

A：我的东西我找得到<u>不就行了嘛</u>！你别在这儿<u>来回翻</u>了！

（四）用所给词语完成对话

Complete the following dialogues with the items provided in the parenthesis

1. （合适吗，请示，随时）

A：你又开你女朋友的车，_____？要不要_____一下？

B：没关系，我的女朋友说，有事_____可以用，可是得负责加油。

2. （本人，不得了嘛）

A：菜都做好了！快点儿来吃吧。

B：小丽，你今天做的菜我都不能吃！

A：为什么？

B：_____现在吃素了。

A：那没关系，这里不是也有青菜吗，你只吃青菜_____。

3. （惊喜，不得了嘛，人家）

A：谁叫你给我买鞋的？我不喜欢这个样子的鞋。

B：_____只是想给你一个_____，没想到你还生气了。

A：你不知道，别人买的鞋，我穿着常常不合适。

B：行了行了，我以后不给你买鞋_____！

4. （终于，折腾）

A：告诉你一件事，我_____找到了一个理想的工作！是香港一家大银行！

B：太好了！我现在出去买鱼、买肉、买青菜，给你做一顿好吃的，好好庆祝一下。

A：别_____了！我们去外边撮一顿吧。

5. （一会儿这样一会儿那样，偶然）

A：我下学期就不想学日文了，日文老师太厉害。

B：你怎么_____的？谁说日文老师厉害？

A：我是在餐厅吃饭_____听到的，听说好几个学生都退课了。

（五）角色扮演 Role play

Make a dialogue with a classmate. One party plays An Qi, and the other plays Ya Ping. Your dialogue should incorporate the provided items.

安琪	亚平
You are upset that your husband has made a mess of the bookshelf that you just organized because he is looking for《史记故事》. If the book is so important，he should buy the book. His way of saving money makes people feel so uncomfortable...	You are almost done writing your newspaper article except for two things that you need to verify in 《史记故事》. You remember that you have a book on the shelf in which you can find the references, but you cannot find it now. At this moment，your wife suggests that you buy《史记故事》，but that's crazy，since the whole set costs over 100 *yuan*. She spends money without a thought.
1. 搞得乱七八糟 2. 瞎折腾 3. 不得了嘛 4. 舍不得 5. 找不着	1. 典故 2. 引用 3. 找不着 4. 就是……也……

■ 三、课堂讨论 Discussion

1. 你认为亚平是一个什么样的人？
2. 安琪是个什么样的人？
3. 亚平应该不应该去书店承认错误？
4. 安琪还应该让她丈夫写篇文章把这件事曝光吗？

第十七课 应 聘

Two Job Interviews

编剧：曾有情

人物 （Characters）

陈燕（Chén Yàn）——女，**盲人钢琴调律师**，三十多岁。

经理 1（jīnglǐ）——男，**琴行经理**，四十多岁。

经理 2（jīnglǐ）——男，**琴行经理**。

课 文 Text

陈　燕：你好！

经理1：你好！

陈　燕：您是这儿的经理吧？

经理1：是是是。

陈　燕：我叫陈燕，是来应聘钢琴**调律**的。

1. 盲人	mángrén	n.	blind person; the blind
2. 钢琴	gāngqín	n.	piano
3. 调律师	tiáolǜshī	n.	piano tuner
4. 琴行	qínháng	n.	piano store
5. 调律	tiáolǜ	v.	tune(a piano)

经 理 1：啊，我知道，坐吧。

陈　燕：谢谢！

经 理 1：怎么样，都调完了？

陈　燕：调完了。

经 理 1：你弹段**曲子**我听听。

陈　燕：嗯，没问题。

　　（画外音：一位**哲人**说过，**兴趣**是最好的老师，我**如愿以偿**[N1]地掌握了钢琴调律这门技术。**于是**，我有了第一次应聘的**经历**。）

　　（Off-screen voice：A wise man once said, passion is one's best teacher. Just as I had wished, I finally mastered the skills in piano tuning, and that gave me my first experience of a job interview.)[①]

经 理 1：非常好，非常好！你的**调琴**手艺非常好，你的**演奏**水平也非常高。

陈　燕：谢谢您**夸奖**。

经 理 1：我们谈一下条件，好吧？我们这儿呢，**试用期**每个月是八百块钱，你觉得怎么样？

6.	曲子	qǔzi	n.	tune; song; melody
7.	哲人	zhérén	n.	sage; man of widsom
8.	兴趣	xìngqù	n.	interest
9.	如愿以偿	rú yuàn yǐ cháng		have one's wishes fulfilled
10.	于是	yúshì	conj.	so; then; thus; as a result
11.	经历	jīnglì	n.	experience
12.	调琴	tiáo qín	vo.	tuning (of pianos)
13.	演奏	yǎnzòu	v.	play (a musical instrument)
14.	夸奖	kuājiǎng	v.	praise; compliment; commend
15.	试用期	shìyòng qī	n.	prebation period

---

①　本课有几段语言较难，我们全文翻译，生词也加了英文翻译，但不一定要求学生记住。

陈　燕：嗯……经理……

经理1：你要有别的什么要求，你也可以提。

陈　燕：您误会了。您给了我这么好的机会，感谢还来不及呢，我没有**理由**提条件。不过——我想告诉您，我是盲人！

经理1：你在**开玩笑**吧？哎，我怎么一点儿看不出来？

陈　燕：我小的时候，我姥姥**培养**的。她要求我像**健全人**一样地和别人**交流**，她**总是**说，健全人能做的我也能做，还要做得更好！

经理1：你的技术确实非常好，不过，你知道，你不可能总是在店**里边调音**，要是没有人带的话，你怎么能找到**用户**呢？我的意思是说，你看**大街上车水马龙**^{N2}的……

陈　燕：谢谢您**关心**，不过——您平时很少听说盲人**出车祸**吧！您知道为什么吗？

经理1：为什么啊？

陈　燕：**俗话**说淹死的全是会水的^{N3}，盲人走路是靠听，所以

16. 理由	lǐyóu	n.	reason; justification
17. 开玩笑	kāi wánxiào	vo.	joke; make fun
18. 培养	péiyǎng	v.	foster; cultivate
19. 健全人	jiànquán rén		healthy person
20. 交流	jiāoliú	v.	communicate
21. 总是	zǒngshì	adv.	always
22. 里边	lǐbian	n.	inside; within
23. 调音	tiáo yīn	vo.	tune the sound (of a piano)
24. 用户	yònghù	n.	consumer
25. 大街	dàjiē	n.	main street
26. 车水马龙	chē shuǐ mǎ lóng		(see note 2)
27. 关心	guānxīn	v.	care; concern (for someone)
28. 出车祸	chū chēhuò	vo.	traffic accident
29. 俗话	súhuà	n.	common saying; proverb

啊……走起路来非常小心谨慎[N4]。

经理1：有道理，行，那这样，明天你来上班。

陈　燕：经理，我想一个月以后来上班行吗？

　　（画外音：我未来的顾客，可能**分布**在北京的每一条大街**小巷**[N5]，我必须能**及时**地找到他们。一个月以后，我几乎**走遍**了北京市的每一个地方，而且，如愿以偿地得到了这**份**工作。当**梦想成真**时，我**唯一**想到的就是**加倍**地**珍惜**[N6]它，就像**健全**的人们珍惜自己的眼睛。几年后，我又**来到**另一家钢琴城应聘。）

（Off-screen voice：My future customers might reside everywhere in Beijing, and I might have to locate them quickly. In a month's time, I had reached almost all corners of the city. As I landed this job, my dream had come true. All I had on my mind was that I should value my job in the same way a healthy person values her own eyes. A few years later, I arrived at a different piano store for another job interview.）

30.	谨慎	jǐnshèn	adj.	prudent; careful; cautious; circumspect
31.	上班	shàng bān	vo.	go to work
32.	分布	fēnbù	v.	distribute (over an area)
33.	小巷	xiǎoxiàng	n.	small alley
34.	及时	jíshí	adj.	timely, in time; promptly
35.	几乎	jīhū	adv.	almost; nearly
36.	遍	biàn	adj.	all over; all around (to be used after a verb as a complement)
37.	份	fèn	m	(a measure word for jobs)
38.	梦想成真	mèng xiǎng chéng zhēn		a dream come true
39.	唯一	wéiyī	adj.	single; only; sole
40.	加倍	jiābèi	adv.	doubly
41.	珍惜	zhēnxī	v.	value; cherish
42.	健全	jiànquán	adj.	healthy; sound
43.	来到	lái dào	vc.	come to; arrive at

陈　燕：经理，行吗？

经理2：想听**实话**吗？在我们这个**行业**中啊，竞争是非常**激烈**的，一般健全的人不一定都能得到这份工作，至于[N7]你嘛，我虽然不能说你是最好的，但你是非常**优秀**的。

经理2：那，你什么时候来上班呢？

陈　燕：对不起，经理，有件事我没跟您说。

经理2：什么事啊？

陈　燕：我现在有工作，我有个同学最近**失业**了，还有许多学钢琴调律的**师弟师妹**们，他们也要毕业了，我是替他们来

应聘的，但您放心，他们肯定能让您**满意**，希望您能给他们一个机会。

经理2：一般人都是**费尽心思**[N8]为自己**求职**应聘，没想到你却替别

44. 实话	shíhuà	n.	truth
45. 行业	hángyè	n.	trade; profession
46. 激烈	jīliè	adj.	intense; acute; fierce
47. 优秀	yōuxiù	adj.	outstanding; excellent
48. 失业	shī yè	vo.	lose one's job; be unemployed
49. 师弟	shīdì	n.	male junior fellow apprentice
50. 师妹	shīmèi	n.	female junior fellow apprentice
51. 毕业	bì yè	vo.	graduate
52. 满意	mǎnyì	adj.	satisfied; pleased
53. 费尽心思	fèi jìn xīnsi		(see note 8)
54. 求职	qiú zhí	vo.	seek employment; apply for a job

人应聘啊，**难能可贵**[N9]啊……行，就冲[N10]你的**为人**，我答应了。

（**画外音**：这就是我两次应聘的故事。朋友们，你们应该相信**阳光**、**色彩**、**世间万物**，在一个盲人**心目中**，比在任何一个健全人的**眼中**都美。我相信，每个盲人都会有属于他自己的**美丽人生**。）

（Off-screen voice：What you have seen is a story of my two job interviews. Believe me, my friends, the sunshine, the colors, and the myriads of things in the world are perhaps even more beautiful in the heart of a blind person than they could ever be in the eyes of someone with healthy vision. Every blind person, as I believe, should be able to have his or her own beautiful life.）

（**字幕**：本**剧根据**盲人钢琴调律师陈燕的**真实**故事**改编**，主人公由陈燕**本人扮演**。）

55. 难能可贵	nán néng kě guì		(see note 9)
56. 为人	wéirén		behavior; conduct
57. 阳光	yángguāng	n.	sunshine
58. 色彩	sècǎi	n.	color
59. 世间	shìjiān	n.	in the world
60. 万物	wànwù	n.	myriads of things
61. 心目中	xīnmù zhōng		in (someone's) mind's eye
62. 眼中	yǎn zhōng		in (someone's) eyes
63. 美丽	měilì	adj.	beautiful
64. 人生	rénshēng	n.	life; human life
65. 字幕	zìmù	n.	caption; subtitle
66. 剧	jù	n.	play
67. 根据	gēnjù	prep.	based on
68. 真实	zhēnshí	adj.	true; real
69. 改编	gǎibiān	v.	adapt
70. 主人公	zhǔréngōng	n.	leading character (in a novel, a play, etc.)
71. 本人	běnrén	n.	himself; herself
72. 扮演	bànyǎn	v.	play the role of

注释 Notes

1. **"如愿以偿"：**

    "愿"的意思是"愿望"，"偿"的意思是"满足"，"如愿以偿"的意思是"愿望得到实现"。

    In the set phrase "如愿以偿"，"愿" stands for "愿望"（wish，hope），and "偿" here means "to fulfill（a wish）". The phrase thus describes one's satisfaction in having his/her wish fulfilled.

2. **"车水马龙"：**

    成语。形容车辆往来，交通繁忙的景象。

    The set phrase "车水马龙" literally means "rivers of carriages and dragons of horses". It is often used to describe the hustling traffic in a city.

3. **"淹死的全是会水的"：**

    俗语。"会水的"就是会游泳的。这个句子的意义是：淹死的人全是会游泳的。用来比喻好逞强的人才容易出问题。

    This popular saying literally means：Those who got drowned all knew well how to swim. Metaphorically it refers to a situation where a person overconfident in his abilities eventually meets his failure.

4. **"小心谨慎"：**

    成语。意思是：人的言语行为非常小心，不马虎急躁。

    This set phrase suggests that one should be discreet and prudent in his words and actions，never perfunctory or impetuous.

    （1）他办事小心谨慎，你放心吧。

    He is prudent in his actions. You can rest assured.

    （2）你这一次马马虎虎，那事情办坏了。以后做事千万小心谨慎。

    You screwed it up this time because you were careless. Be sure to be prudent in the future.

    （3）我小心谨慎地做每一件事，从来没出过问题。

    I am circumspect in doing everything，and have never caused any problem.

(4) 他是一个小心谨慎的人。

He is a very discreet person.

5. **大街小巷**：

"大街"指城市里大的街道，小巷指城市里的小巷子、小胡同。

In the set phrase "大街小巷"，"大街" literally refers to main streets and "小巷" to small alleys and lanes. The phrase simply means "everywhere" in the city.

6. **"加倍珍惜"**：

"加倍"表示"比原来的程度深得多"，"加倍珍惜"的意思是"比以前珍惜得多得多"。

Here "加倍" means "doubly" or "to a much larger extent than before". The phrase "加倍珍惜" thus means "to cherish（something）much more dearly than before".

7. **"至于"**：

连词"至于"用于一段话的开头，其作用是把这一段话和前边的句子连接起来。用"至于"连接的的句子语意上与前面的句子有联系。

The conjunction "至于" leads a sentence or a passage and links it up with the foregoing one. What follows "至于" is in some way relevant to the sentence or passage prior to it.

(1) 在我们这个行业中啊，竞争是非常激烈的，一般健全的人不一定都能得到这份工作，至于你嘛，我虽然不能说你是最好的，但你是非常优秀的。

In our trade，competition is acute. It would be difficult even for a healthy person to land this job. As for you，although I can't say you are the very best，you are certainly outstanding.

(2) 我们先商量一下周末去不去旅行，至于去什么地方，一会儿再讨论。

Let's first decide whether we will travel or not this weekend. As for the destination，we will discuss it later.

(3) 老张现在可以休假，至于小李，不能休假，都休假了，谁工作呀？

Old Zhang can take his vacation now. As for Young Li，he can't at this point. If everybody leaves for vacation，who will be working?

8. **"费尽心思"**：

成语。意思是：想尽办法，想了一切办法。有一些贬义。

This set phrase means "to rack one's brains（in scheming for something)". It is usually used in a somewhat negative sense.

(1) 一般人都是费尽心思，为自己求职应聘，没想到你却替别人应聘啊，难能可贵啊……行，就冲你的为人，我答应了。

Most people would beat their brains to find a job for themselves. Who would think that you would apply for a job on someone else's behalf? That's something truly commendable... OK，because of your exemplary conduct，I'll meet your request.

(2) 为了把女朋友再抢回来，他费尽了心思。

In order to win his girlfriend back，he has resorted to every means.

(3) 他费尽心思地找到了一个工作，没想到那个公司很快就倒闭了。

It took him great pains to find this job，but who would know that company should go bankrupt so soon.

9. **"难能可贵"：**

成语。意思是：很难做到的事竟然做到了，是非常可贵的。

The meaning of this set phrase is as follows：What was difficult to achieve became actually achieved，which was therefore remarkable and commendable.

(1) 一般人都是费尽心思，为自己求职应聘，没想到你却替别人应聘，难能可贵啊……行，就冲你的为人，我答应了。

Most people would beat their brains to find a job for themselves. Who would think that you would apply for a job on someone else's behalf? That's something truly commendable... OK，because of your exemplary conduct，I'll meet your request.

(2) 更加难能可贵的是，他受了伤以后还救了好几个人。

Even more laudable was the fact that he rescued several other people after he had been injured.

(3) 你过去对他那么不好，现在他这样帮助你，这是难能可贵的。

You didn't treat him well in the past，but he is being so helpful to you now. That's something really commendable.

10. **"冲"：**

介词"冲"有"根据""凭着"的意思。口语。

In colloquial speech, the preposition "冲" can be used in the sense of "based on" or "because of".

(1) 行，就冲你的为人，我答应了。

OK，because of your exemplary conduct，I'll meet your request.

（2）就冲她这个努力劲儿，一定能考上一个好大学。

With such diligence on her part，she will certainly be able to get into a good college.

（3）就冲你这句话，这件事我答应了。

Based on these words of yours，you have my promise on this matter.

听说练习 Listening & Speaking Exercises

一、课文理解 Text Comprehension

（一）根据故事情节选择适当的答案
Please choose the most appropriate answer based on the story

1. 陈燕为什么去这家钢琴店？（　　）
   A. 弹段曲子　　　　　B. 应聘工作　　　　　C. 演奏钢琴

2. 陈燕的调琴手艺非常好是因为她（　　）
   A. 对钢琴调律有兴趣
   B. 认为钢琴调律好找工作
   C. 认为钢琴调律对盲人合适

3. 经理给了她这份工作，但是担心她（　　）
   A. 嫌钱太少
   B. 开车出事
   C. 在街上走不安全

4. 每个月是八百块钱，陈燕觉得怎么样？（　　）
   A. 够多了　　　　　B. 不够多　　　　　C. 很高兴

5. 盲人走起路来非常（　　）
   A. 费尽心思　　　　　B. 梦想成真　　　　　C. 小心谨慎

6. 在陈燕看来，健全的人最应该珍惜的是（　　）
   A. 自己的姥姥　　　　　B. 自己的眼睛　　　　　C. 自己的工作

7. 第二位经理认为像陈燕这样的人（　　）
   A. 难能可贵　　　　　B. 小心谨慎　　　　　C. 费尽心思

（二）根据课文判断下面句子意思的正误
State whether the following statements are true or false based on the story

1.（　　）陈燕的调琴手艺非常好，而且她的演奏水平也非常高。

2.（　　）陈燕应聘过两次，两次她都为自己找到了工作。

3. (　　) 陈燕学习钢琴调律是为了生活。

4. (　　) 据陈燕说，盲人走路出事故的不多。

5. (　　) 俗话说淹死的人都是不会游泳的。

6. (　　) 因为陈燕一看就是个盲人，所以工作好找。

7. (　　) 现在找钢琴调律的工作不太容易，竞争非常激烈。

8. (　　) 陈燕第二次应聘又成功了，因为她是应聘的人里最好的。

（三）先听故事叙述，然后复述故事
Listen to the narrative first and then retell the story

陈燕是位盲人，她姥姥告诉她，健全人能做的她也一定能做，还要做得更好。

陈燕对钢琴调律这门技术很有兴趣，学得非常好。听说有一家钢琴店要聘请一位钢琴调律师，她就去应聘了。由于她不但调琴手艺好，而且演奏水平也非常高，所以经理立刻聘用了她。她为自己能有这个工作机会而非常高兴。经理担心路上人多车多她走路不安全，她却说因为盲人看不见路，所以走路非常小心，像她这样的人反而很少出事。

陈燕非常珍惜她的工作。在这家钢琴店工作了几年后，她又来到另一家钢琴城应聘，这一次是替她的一个最近失业的同学和师弟师妹们来应聘的。经理认为，现在 一般人都费尽心思为自己求职应聘，而陈燕这样做，实在是难能可贵，就答应了她的要求。

■ 二、词语使用 Application of Vocabulary and Grammar

（一）选择题
Choose the item that is grammatically correct

1. 我叫陈燕，是_____应聘钢琴调律的。

　　A. 会　　　　　　　　B. 来　　　　　　　　C. 能

2. 我们谈_____条件，好吧？

　　A. 一下　　　　　　　B. 一些　　　　　　　C. 一个

3. 你是盲人？你在开玩笑吧？我怎么一点儿看不_____？

　　A. 起来　　　　　　　B. 上来　　　　　　　C. 出来

4. 经理，您平时很少听说盲人_____车祸吧！您知道为什么吗？

　　A. 出　　　　　　　　B. 有　　　　　　　　C. 撞

5. 盲人走路是靠听，胆子小，所以啊走起路＿＿＿＿非常小心谨慎。

    A. 来   B. 上   C. 很

6. 我今天是＿＿＿＿一个最近失业了的同学来应聘的。

    A. 跟   B. 替   D. 给

（二）选择题

Circle the answer that best reflects the meaning of the underlined portion of the sentence

1. 俗话说淹死的全是<u>会水</u>的。（   ）

    A. 会喝水

    B. 会游泳

    C. 水很多

    D. 在水里头

2. 一般人都是费尽心思，为自己求职应聘，没想到你却替别人应聘啊，<u>难能可贵</u>啊……（   ）

    A. 非常可贵

    B. 又难又贵

    C. 难了就贵

    D. 能难就贵

3. 一个月以后，我几乎<u>走遍了北京市的每一个地方</u>。（   ）

    A. 北京市的每一个地方都走熟了

    B. 北京市的每一个地方都要走

    C. 北京市的每一个地方都去了

    D. 北京市的每一个地方都走过一遍

4. 你看大街上<u>车水马龙</u>的……（   ）

    A. 人、车很多

    B. 有马有龙

    C. 什么都有

    D. 乱七八糟

5. 您误会了，您给了我这么好的机会，<u>感谢还来不及</u>呢，我没有理由提条件。（   ）

    A. 我忘了感谢

    B. 说感谢还怕说得太晚

C. 感谢不好

    D. 感谢不了

6. 兴趣是最好的老师，我<u>如愿以偿</u>地掌握了钢琴调律这门技术。（　　）

    A. 实现了愿望

    B. 为愿望付出代价

    C. 像愿望一样

    D. 补偿自己的愿望

（三）选择适当的词语，替换句中的画线部分

Choose the most appropriate words to replace the underlined parts

A. 费尽心思	B. 如愿以偿	C. 误会
D. 冲	E. 车水马龙	F. 分布在……

1. 我非常想当钢琴调律师，今天<u>终于当上了</u>。

2. 您<u>弄错我的意思了</u>。您给了我这么好的机会，感谢还来不及呢，我没有理由提条件。

3. 北京的大街上<u>人很多车也很多</u>，过马路得小心。

4. 我的顾客，<u>北京的每一条大街小巷都有</u>。

5. 一般人都是<u>想很多办法</u>，为自己求职应聘，没想到你却替别人应聘啊，难能可贵啊……

6. 就<u>只因为</u>你的为人，我答应了。

（四）用所给词语完成对话

Complete the following dialogues with the items provided in the parenthesis

1. （至于，一趟）

    A：我们今年夏天一起去欧洲旅行_____，怎么样？

    B：欧洲很大，去哪个国家？

    A：先说你想不想去，_____去什么地方，再商量。

2. （小心谨慎，费尽心思）

    A：好久没见老张了，她是不是在休假？

    B：他最近为了给他女儿找工作，_____，腿都跑断了。

    A：他是一个_____的人，不会做不该做的事情吧？

3. （冲……，难能可贵，加倍珍惜）

    A：上个月陈燕替我找到了一份工作，我后来才知道她也已经失业好几个月了，她这样做，真是_____。

    B：你得到这个工作不容易，经理是_____陈燕的为人才答应给你这份工作的。

A：我会_____的。

4.（误会，确实）

经理：怎么不说话？一个月八百元你是不是觉得少了点儿？

陈燕：您_____了，我是高兴得不知说什么好了！

经理：一个月八百元_____不太多，但这是试用期工资。

（五）角色扮演 Role play

Make a dialogue with a classmate. One party plays Chen Yan，and the other plays the Manager. Your dialogue should incorporate the provided items.

陈燕	经理
You come to a piano store for an interview for a position as a piano tuner. You introduce yourself to the manager and inform him the reason for being at his store. After having tuned a piano，the manager asks you to play a piece of music. He is impressed and you thank him for his praises. He makes an offer to you but worries about your safety while traveling on your job. You convince him that there are fewer accidents involving blind people than with those who have sight.	You are very impressed by the skills and the music talent of the job seeker. You are even more surprised to learn that she is actually blind. You offer her the job and inform her of the salary. Since she does not respond quickly, you think she might not be happy with the pay. The fact is that she was too happy to thank you quickly enough. She puts your mind at ease when you tell her of your worry about her safety as the job requires going to customers' houses and this would be difficult for a blind person.
1. 应聘　　 2. 钢琴调律 3. 夸奖　　 4. 误会 5. 来不及　 6. 健全人 7. 淹死的全是会水的 8. 小心谨慎	1. 弹段曲子　 2. 调琴手艺 3. 演奏水平　 4. 条件 5. 试用期　　 6. 要求 7. 开玩笑　　 8. 车水马龙 9. 有道理

■ 三、课堂讨论 Discussion

1. 陈燕得到她的第一份工作时，非常感谢那位经理给了她一个这么好的工作机会。当经理问他有没有什么条件想提的时候，她说她没有理由提条件。你对她这句话有什么看法？

2. 经理冲陈燕的为人答应把她得到的工作给她失业的同学或师弟师妹们做。要是你是这位经理，你会这样做吗？为什么？

第十八课 闲 话

Gossip

编剧：曾有情

人物 （Characters）

刘五 （Liú Wǔ）——男，四十多岁，京郊农民。

周嫂 （Zhōu sǎo）——四十多岁，京郊农民。

朱琴 （Zhū Qín）——女，二十多岁，京郊农民。

周嫂女儿 （Zhōu sǎo nǚ'ér）

课 文 Text

刘　五：周嫂。

周　嫂：是刘五啊。

刘　五：回村啊？上车吧，我捎你回去。

周　嫂：哎哟，刘五，你看看我……我还真有福气啊。怎么着，又

1. 闲话	xiánhuà	n.	gossip
2. 京郊	Jīngjiāo	N.	suburbs or outskirts of Beijing
3. 农民	nóngmín	n.	peasant
4. 村	cūn	n.	village
5. 福气	fúqi	n.	good luck; good fortune

上北京**办货**去了啊？

刘　五：这两天这**小卖部**不是卖得好嘛。

周　嫂：是啊。

刘　五：哎，对了，**嫂子**啊。我今儿上北京看见**新闻**了。

周　嫂：新闻？

刘　五：**爆炸性**新闻。

周　嫂：啊，快说说，啥新闻呀？

刘　五：知道咱村上北京**打工**去那老**孟**家那大**小子**[N1]孟刚？

周　嫂：知道。

刘　五：我今儿在北京看见他**搂**着一姑娘，那姑娘，**腰**还挺细，姑娘那**脑袋**靠在小伙子**肩膀**上，**好家伙**，**陶醉**那劲儿[N2]。

周　嫂：哎，你真看着了？你可**瞅准**了啊。

---

6. 办货	bàn huò	vo.	purchase or buy goods wholesale
7. 小卖部	xiǎomàibù	n.	small shop; convenience store
8. 嫂（子）	sǎo（zi）	n.	elder brother's wife (a respectful form of address for a woman who is usually older than the speaker); elder sister-in-law
9. 新闻	xīnwén	n.	news; rumor
10. 爆炸性	bàozhàxìng	n.	explosive; unexpected
11. 打工	dǎ gōng	vo.	have a temporary job; do manual work
12. 孟	Mèng	N.	(a surname)
13. 小子	xiǎozi	n.	boy; chap
14. 搂	lǒu	v.	hold in one's arms; hug; embrace
15. 腰	yāo	n.	waist; small of the back
16. 脑袋	nǎodai	n.	head
17. 肩膀	jiānbǎng	n.	shoulder
18. 好家伙	hǎo jiāhuo		(see note 2)
19. 陶醉	táozuì	v.	be intoxicated (with happiness)
20. 准	zhǔn	adj.	accurate; exact

刘　五：我这玩儿鹰的眼睛我能看不准吗？

周　嫂：哎哟，那朱琴马上就要和孟刚结婚了，哎，这要是真的的话，朱琴还**蒙在鼓里**N3呢。唉，朱琴呀，可是咱们村里的**一朵花**，哪个姑娘能**比得上**人家姑娘漂亮啊？

刘　五：漂不漂亮我是没看清楚。

周　嫂：唉，我闺女呀和孟刚在一个公司打工，听我闺女说啊，孟刚这小伙子，特**招**女孩儿喜欢，**瞧瞧**，这不是，**闹出事**来了吧？

刘　五：对了，嫂子，你**舌头**长N4，可别到处给我说去。

周　嫂：瞧你说的……

周　嫂：哎，朱琴，上哪儿去？

朱　琴：周婶，我去孟刚家，他们家有活儿，我得帮把手N5去。

周　嫂：哎哟，我的傻姑娘啊，你还去他们家干的哪门子活儿呀？N6

21.	鹰	yīng	n.	eagle; falcon
22.	蒙在鼓里	méng zài gǔ li		be kept in the dark
23.	朵	duǒ	m.	measure word for flowers
24.	比得上	bǐ de shàng	vc.	compare; compete
25.	招	zhāo	v.	attract
26.	瞧瞧	qiáo qiao		look; see
27.	闹出事	nào chū shì		be in trouble; have an accident
28.	舌头	shétou	n.	tongue
29.	婶	shěn	n.	aunt (a respectful address to a woman about one's mother's age)
30.	干活儿	gàn huór	vo.	work; labor

朱　琴：周婶，我和孟刚很快就是一家人了……

周　婶：我知道，我周婶不是看着你从小长大的吗？

朱　琴：周婶，怎么了？

周　嫂：哦，没事，没事……哎，不过朱琴啊，不是我爱拉闲话[N7]，你可得**留点儿神**，孟刚啊，可不是个什么好东西。

朱　琴：到底怎么了？

周　嫂：哎，我跟你说啊……

朱　琴：刘五哥，我问你个事。

刘　五：啊，看你这**表情**，我就知道你要问啥，周嫂她都告诉你了？

朱　琴：你真的看到了吗？

刘　五：啊。

女　儿：妈。

周　嫂：哟，闺女，回来了？

女　儿：我跟孟刚一块儿回来的。

周　嫂：哟，闺女，你怎么跟他**打联联**[N8]了，我可告诉你啊，他这人不**正经**。

女　儿：妈，您是不是老**毛病**又犯了？

周　嫂：没有啊，我最近啊这个**胃**特**争气**，一次也没疼过。

31.	留点儿神	liú diǎnr shén		be careful；be mindful
32.	表情	biǎoqíng	n.	(facial) expression
33.	打联联	dǎliánlián	v.	associate with someone
34.	正经	zhèngjing	adj.	decent；respectable
35.	毛病	máobìng	n.	disease；illness；shortcoming (a fault in sb's character)
36.	胃	wèi	n.	stomach
37.	争气	zhēng qì	vo.	don't let down

女　儿：我是说您这嘴！您怎么知道孟刚不正经啊？

周　嫂：你刘五哥**亲眼**所见，**要不是**你妈我**心眼儿**好啊，他那没**过门**的**媳妇儿**这下可就**惨**了！

女　儿：敢情这事跟您有关系啊？您知道吗？这事您可闹大发[N9]了，人家朱琴姐差点儿把结婚证给撕了。我这次回来，就是专门陪孟刚**辟谣**的。

周　嫂：辟谣？你辟什么谣啊？

女　儿：妈——那天，我在**街**上**突然肾结石**犯了。

周　嫂：啊。

女　儿：疼得都快**虚脱**了，孟刚**搀**的是我，要不是他把我送医院，我还不知道怎么样了呢。

周　嫂：啊？

周　嫂：哎，刘五。

刘　五：哎呦，周嫂。

38. 亲眼	qīnyǎn	adv.	(see) with one's own eyes；(witness) personally
39. 要不是	yàobushì	conj.	if it were not for
40. 心眼儿	xīnyǎnr	n.	intention; heart
41. 过门	guò mén	vo.	(of a woman)get married into the husband's family
42. 媳妇儿	xífur	n.	wife(northern colloq.)
43. 惨	cǎn	adj.	miserable; tragic
44. 辟谣	pì yáo	vo.	refute a rumor
45. 街	jiē	n.	street
46. 突然	tūrán	adj.	suddenly; unexpectedly
47. 肾结石	shènjiéshí	n.	kidney stone
48. 虚脱	xūtuō	v.	collapse
49. 搀	chān	v.	assist by the arm

周　嫂：就那天就你那通**胡嘞嘞**[N10]，害得我是**猪八戒**照镜子——里外不是人[N11]。

刘　五：嗨，您甭说别的了，我这不也让村里人给**唾沫**星子**淹死**了[N12]吗。

周　嫂：唉，都怪我这张**乌鸦嘴**[N13]，**搬弄是非**[N14]，把我闺女的**救命恩人**呀，都给坑了。

刘　五：**可不是吗**，咱净**顾**自个儿嘴**痛快**了[N15]，这边把人家孟刚**名誉**给**毁**了，那边，也对不起朱琴呐。

周　嫂：可不是吗，这不，我刚去了孟刚家，又是**赔不是**，又是感谢，这会儿呀，我正要去朱琴家给人家**赔礼道歉**呀。

刘　五：咱**想一块儿去了**[N16]啊，我也是去道歉去的。

50.	胡嘞嘞	húlēle	v.	speak nonsense; nonsense
51.	猪八戒	Zhū Bājiè	N.	(see note 11)
52.	唾沫	tuòmo	n.	saliva; spittle (see note 12)
53.	淹死	yān sǐ	vc.	be drowned
54.	乌鸦嘴	wūyā zuǐ		(see note 13)
55.	搬弄是非	bānnòng shìfēi		(see note 14)
56.	救命恩人	jiùmìng ēnrén		savior
57.	坑	kēng	v.	ruin (as used in this story); entrap
58.	可不是	kěbushì	adv.	(I) can't agree with you more; I totally agree with you
59.	顾	gù	v.	care for
60.	自个儿	zìgěr	pron.	oneself; by oneself
61.	痛快	tòng·kuài	adj.	to one's heart's content; to one's great satisfaction
62.	名誉	míngyù	n.	reputation; fame
63.	毁	huǐ	v.	damage; ruin
64.	赔不是	péi búshì	vo.	apologize
65.	赔礼道歉	péi lǐ dào qiàn		apologize
66.	想一块儿去了	xiǎng yíkuàir qu le		(see note 16)

注释 Notes

1. "老孟家那大小子":

"老孟家"就是"姓孟的家",北方人很喜欢这样说。"大小子"就是"大儿子"。口语。

"老孟家" means "the Meng family". This expression "老×家" is used commonly in the Northeast area. "大小子" refers to the oldest son, a colloquial expression.

2. "好家伙,陶醉那劲儿":

"好家伙",表示惊叹或赞叹,用于感叹句。

"好家伙", an exclamation, meaning "My goodness!" It is used to express one's surprise.

(1) 我今儿在北京看到他搂着一姑娘,那姑娘,腰还挺细,姑娘那脑袋靠在小伙子肩膀上,好家伙,陶醉那劲儿。

I came across him holding a girl in his arms in Beijing today. The girl had a slender waist, and was laying her head on his shoulder. I don't believe I've seen a more blissful couple!

(2) 我刚才上了一趟街,好家伙,人那个多呀!

I just went shopping. You wouldn't believe how many people there were!

(3) 我们全班都出来找你,好家伙,原来你在这儿玩儿电子游戏呢!

The whole class was out looking for you. And you've been here playing computer games all along! Unbelievable!

3. "蒙在鼓里":

"蒙"的意思是"遮盖"。"蒙在鼓里"就是"被蒙在鼓里",比喻什么都不知道。"蒙" means "to cover". "蒙在鼓里" means "to be kept in the dark".

4. 舌头长:

比喻爱说闲话。口语。

"舌头长", an idiomatic expression, is commonly used to refer to someone who loves to gossip.

5. **帮把手**：

　　帮助一下。口语。

　　"to lend a hand"，a colloquial term，same as "帮助一下".

6. **"你还去他家干哪门子活儿啊"**：

　　意思是：为什么还去他家干活？这是个反问句，意思是：不应该还去他家干活。

　　"What are you going to his house for?" Through this rhetorical question，the speaker is trying to suggest that she should not go to his house to help.

7. **"拉闲话"**：

　　意思是"说闲话"。口语。

　　It is an idiomatic expression meaning "to gossip".

8. **"打联联"**：

　　意思是"经常来往"，有一点儿贬义。

　　"to associate with someone"，it has some derogative sense.

9. **"大发"**：

　　意思是"超过适当的限度，过分"。口语。

　　An idiomatic expression，meaning "overdo".

　　"闹大发了" means "to be in deep trouble"，"to mess up big".

10. **"胡嘞嘞"**：

　　随便乱说。口语。

　　To speak nonsense. A colloquial term.

11. **"猪八戒照镜子——里外不是人"**：

　　歇后语。字面的意思是：猪八戒照镜子，镜子里边外边都是猪八戒，是猪，不是人。这个歇后语用来比喻一个人做了一件事，得罪了各个方面的人。

　　This is an enigmatic folk simile. Its literal meaning is "The Pig (one of the characters in the novel *Journey to the West*) looks in the mirror. No matter how he looks at his reflection and at himself，he still looks ugly." This simile is used here to refer to someone who offends and is，therefore，disliked by everybody.

12. **"让……唾沫星子淹死了"**：

　　"唾沫"就是"唾液"，"星子"比喻细小、细碎的东西。"唾沫星子"

指说话时从嘴里喷出的细小的唾液。口语。全句比喻遭到很多人指责、唾骂。

"唾沫星子" refers to the saliva that one spits out when speaking excitedly. This is a very colloquial expression，meaning that someone is furiously criticized by everyone (so much that she/he could be drowned by the saliva from so many people).

13. **"乌鸦嘴"：**

比喻人说不吉利的话。口语。

"Crow's mouth" is used here as a metaphor to refer to someone who always says bad things about others. It is used in colloquial speech.

14. **"搬弄是非"：**

意思是在背后传闲话，挑拨离间，引起纠纷。

"搬弄是非" means to spread rumors, or tells tales to make issues or cause disputes.

15. **"净顾自个儿嘴痛快了"：**

"净"的意思是"只"；"自个儿"是"自己"；"嘴痛快"意思是"因为说什么而使自己高兴"。口语。

"净" means "only"；"自个儿" is "oneself", used in colloquial speech. The whole sentence is "One says something just for the pleasure of saying it without considering the consequences."

16. **"咱想一块儿去了"：**

意思是"（对某事）咱们的想法一样"。

We are thinking of the same thing.

听说练习　Listening & Speaking Exercises

■ 一、课文理解 Text Comprehension

（一）根据故事情节选择适当的答案

Please choose the most appropriate answer based on the story

1. 刘五到北京_____去了。

   A. 打工　　　　　　B. 看新闻　　　　　　C. 买东西

2. 孟刚（　　）

   A. 很受女孩子欢迎　B. 很喜欢女孩子　　　C. 在北京有一个女朋友

3. 刘五知道周嫂（　　）

   A. 喜欢孟刚　　　　B. 喜欢说闲话　　　　C. 不喜欢朱琴

4. 周嫂（　　）

   A. 早就认识朱琴　　B. 刚认识朱琴　　　　C. 最近认识了朱琴

5. 周嫂觉得朱琴不应该去孟刚家帮忙，因为她以为朱琴（　　）

   A. 很傻　　　　　　B. 受骗了　　　　　　C. 太漂亮了

6. 周嫂的女儿从北京回来是为了（　　）

   A. 看周嫂　　　　　B. 辟谣　　　　　　　C. 陪孟刚

7. 村里的人都说（　　）

   A. 刘五做得对

   B. 刘五不应该去北京

   C. 刘五做得不对

8. 周嫂去给孟刚（　　）

   A. 赔钱　　　　　　B. 送礼　　　　　　　C. 赔礼道歉

（二）根据课文判断下面句子意思的正误

State whether the following statements are true or false based on the story

1. （　　）刘五跟周嫂一起去北京了。

2.（　　）孟刚爱上了周嫂的女儿。

3.（　　）朱琴就要跟孟刚结婚了。

4.（　　）周嫂担心朱琴吃亏。

5.（　　）周嫂的女儿怪妈妈不应该说闲话。

6.（　　）刘五不后悔说闲话。

（三）先听故事叙述，然后复述故事

Listen to the narrative first and then retell the story

　　刘五去北京办货回来的时候碰到了周嫂，他顺路把周嫂带回家。他们在路上聊天的时候，刘五把他在北京看到孟刚的事情告诉了周嫂。孟刚是他们村里最帅的小伙子，下个月就要跟漂亮姑娘朱琴举行婚礼了。可是，刘五看见他搂着别的姑娘在路上走。周嫂听了很吃惊，很快就告诉了朱琴。朱琴听了周嫂的话，哭着要把结婚证撕了。

　　实际上那天是周嫂的女儿得了急病，孟刚送她去医院。周嫂的女儿和孟刚听说这件事以后，赶忙从北京回来辟谣，孟刚和朱琴这一对年轻人的婚姻才没有被闲话给毁了。

■ 二、词语使用 Application of Vocabulary and Grammar

（一）选择题

Choose the item that is grammatically correct

1. 他打网球打得特别好，我认识的人里没有一个能_____他的。

    A. 比　　　　　　B. 比得上　　　　C. 比赛　　　　D. 争气

2. 明天我搬家，你能不能来帮_____手？

    A. 个　　　　　　B. 次　　　　　　C. 把　　　　　D. 只

3. 圆圆的爸爸错怪了圆圆，觉得很对不起她，_____去学校给圆圆道歉。

    A. 顺路　　　　　B. 亲眼　　　　　C. 敢情　　　　D. 专门

4. 他们周末老是开晚会，闹到很晚，你看看，_____出事儿来了吧？

    A. 坑　　　　　　B. 闹　　　　　　C. 蒙　　　　　D. 办

5. _____，你明天又要有考试了？连饭都不吃了！

    A. 怎么着　　　　B. 留点儿神　　　C. 可不是吗　　D. 瞧瞧

6. 我的同屋_____顾自己高兴，每天一回来就边听边唱，害得我没办法准备考试。我真想这两天住在图书馆不回宿舍了。

A. 敢情　　　B. 犯　　　　　C. 净　　　D. 专门

（二）选择题

Circle the answer that best reflects the meaning of the sentence

1. 这两天小卖部不是卖得好嘛。（　　　）

 A. 这两天小卖部卖的东西很好。

 B. 这两天小卖部的生意很好。

 C. 这两天小卖部卖不出去东西。

 D. 这两天小卖部卖东西卖得不多。

2. 朱琴可是咱们村里的一朵花，哪个姑娘能比得上人家姑娘漂亮啊？

（　　　）

 A. 朱琴虽然很漂亮，可是她没有那家人的姑娘漂亮。

 B. 朱琴像花一样漂亮，别的姑娘都喜欢跟她比。

 C. 朱琴漂亮是漂亮，可是有一个姑娘比她更漂亮。

 D. 朱琴是我们村里最漂亮的姑娘，没有一个姑娘比她漂亮。

3. 你还去他们家干的哪门子活儿呀？（　　　）

 A. 你为什么还去他家帮忙？

 B. 你为什么还去他家住？

 C. 你知道他们家在哪儿吗？

 D. 你不应该还去他家干活儿。

4. 不是我爱拉闲话，你可得留点儿神。（　　　）

 A. 我不喜欢说闲话，你知道。

 B. 你不要以为我这是喜欢说闲话，我劝你一定要小心一点儿。

 C. 我不想跟你瞎说，可是你得注意一点儿。

 D. 我不喜欢说闲话，你也别听。

5. 敢情这件事跟你有关系啊？（　　　）

 A. 你是怎么知道这件事的？

 B. 你怎么能知道这件事？

 C. 我真没有想到原来这件事跟你有关系！

 D. 我真没有想到你这么没有感情！

6. 可不是吗，他们差一点儿就把孟刚的名誉给毁了。（　　　）

 A. 我完全同意你说的话，他们差一点儿就坏了孟刚的名誉。

 B. 真是的，他们差一点儿就给孟刚找了一个大麻烦。

C. 不是这样，他们已经坏了孟刚的名誉。

D. 这是怎么话说的，他们为什么要给孟刚找这么大的麻烦？

7. 都是我这张乌鸦嘴，害得我是猪八戒照镜子——里外不是人。（　　）

   A. 都是因为我说话说得太多，别人都不喜欢我。

   B. 都是因为我说话说得不好听，别人都说我的嘴长得像乌鸦。

   C. 都是因为我的嘴不好看，别人说我像猪八戒。

   D. 都是因为我瞎说，现在我家里人和外边的人都说我不对。

（三）选择适当的词语，替换句中的画线部分

Choose the most appropriate words to replace the underlined parts

> A. 可不是吗　B. 怎么着　　C. 留点儿神　　D. 我们想到一块儿去了
> E. 赔礼道歉　F. 蒙在鼓里　G. 那可不是嘛　H. 留点儿神　I. 帮把手

1. A：我想今年夏天打工挣钱，明年夏天去中国学习。

  B：真的啊，<u>我也是这样想的</u>，那我们明年可以一起去。

2. A：<u>怎么样</u>？还在做功课哪？

  B：<u>对呀</u>，我的功课比你们的多得多。

3. A：这张桌子很重，<u>我来帮个忙</u>！

  B：谢谢！哎，<u>小心一点儿</u>，别撞着你。

4. A：听说张天明现在有一个女朋友，她叫丽莎，是个美国女孩儿。

  B：是吗？他爸爸一定还<u>不知道</u>呢。要是他爸爸知道了，一定不同意，因为他总让张天明找一个文化背景差不多的女孩儿。

  A：那咱们跟他爸爸说话的时候可得<u>小心一点儿</u>。

5. A：不管是大人还是孩子，对别人做错了事，都得<u>认错</u>。

  B：<u>这是肯定的</u>。

（四）用所给词语完成对话

Complete the following dialogues with the items provided in the parenthesis

1.（搬弄是非，这下可……，赔礼道歉，）

  A：你听说了吗？朱琴差点儿跟孟刚分手。

  B：听说了，都是因为周嫂_____。后来，她跟刘五一起去朱琴和孟刚家_____了！她_____知道说闲话的"好处"了。

2.（可不是吗，想到一块儿去了）

  A：今天考完试，第一件事就是回宿舍睡觉，然后得去洗衣服。

  B：_____！大家都会去洗衣服，我们得早一点儿去。

A：我们＿＿＿＿＿＿＿。

3.（怎么着，可不是吗）

A：＿＿＿＿＿＿，我们走吧！

B：我们等你呢！是不是有点儿晚了？

B：＿＿＿＿＿＿，我们得快一点儿了！

4.（蒙在鼓里，留点儿神）

A：他知道自己得癌症了吗？

B：大家都没告诉他，他还＿＿＿＿＿＿。所以你跟他说话的时候＿＿＿＿＿＿。

（五）角色扮演 Role play

Make a dialogue with a classmate. One party plays Zhou sao, and the other plays Zhou sao's daughter. Your dialogue should incorporate the provided items.

周嫂	女儿
You are very surprised to see your daughter back home from Beijing, and even more surprised to hear that she came back with Meng Gang.	You couldn't believe that your mom was involved in spreading the rumor. It was Meng Gang who saved your life. The reason you came back was so you could end the rumor, and let everyone know the truth.
1. 怎么跟他…… 2. 不正经 3. 要不是……这下可就……	1. 你怎么知道…… 2. 敢情…… 3. 专门 4. 辟谣 5. 要不是……我……

■ 三、课堂讨论 Discussion

1. 你觉得周嫂心眼儿好吗？

2. 如果你是朱琴，你信不信周嫂的话？

3. 为什么一些人喜欢说闲话？

4. 你周围有喜欢说闲话的人吗？如果有，请你说说他的故事。

第十九课 别露怯

Don't Make a Fool of Yourself

编剧：刘艳

人物 (Characters)

爸爸 (bàba) ——四十多岁。

妈妈 (māma) ——四十出头儿。

翎子 (Língzi) ——女儿，十六岁。

课 文 Text

翎　子：慢慢走……不错不错。

爸　爸：哟，你们俩这演什么戏呢？

翎　子：我在教老妈美姿美仪[N1]呢！

爸　爸：你妈平时就挺美的，倒是你呀，太爱臭美了。

翎　子：哎呀，您不懂！

---

1. 露怯	lòu qiè	vo.	(see note 5)
2. 出头儿	chūtóur		slightly over... in age
3. 翎子	Língzi	N.	a person's given name
4. 老妈	lǎomā	n.	(a colloquial form of address for mother)
5. 美姿美仪	měi zī měi yí		(see note 1)
6. 臭美	chòuměi	v.	showy; indulged in making-up

爸　爸：说起来^{N2}臭美，我倒想起来了。翎子妈，翎子她妈……

妈　妈：哎！

爸　爸：给我找一身穿得出去^{N3}的**行头**，明天我跟**外宾**要谈判。

妈　妈：哎！

爸　爸：翎子啊！

翎　子：哎。

爸　爸：你这学**外事**服务的，爸爸今天有个问题要**请教**你。

翎　子：说吧，是不是关于臭美的问题呀？

爸　爸：西餐怎么吃？

翎　子：怎么吃？用嘴吃吧。

爸　爸：我还不知道用嘴吃……我是说这里边有什么讲究没有，**省得**^{N4}我明天跟人吃饭时露怯^{N5}。

翎　子：讲究当然有啦，可我也不能白教您啊，是不是？至于这个**学费**问题嘛……

爸　爸：这孩子还真有经济头脑啊，说吧，多少钱？别太黑^{N6}喽。

翎　子：不黑不黑，只要你请妈和我也去**西餐厅**吃顿西餐就行了。

爸　爸：边**实践**边学习^{N7}，行。

　　　（画外音：她爸，试试这**西装**来。）

爸　爸：哎。

7. 一身	yì shēn		whole body；(combination of) everything one wears
8. 行头	xíngtou	n.	clothing；costume
9. 外宾	wàibīn	n.	foreign guest；foreign visitor
10. 外事	wàishì	n.	foreign affairs
11. 请教	qǐngjiào	v.	consult；seek advice from
12. 省得	shěngde	v.	(see note 4)
13. 学费	xuéfèi	n.	tuition fee
14. 西餐厅	xīcāntīng	n.	Western-style restaurant
15. 实践	shíjiàn	n./v.	practice
16. 西装	xīzhuāng	n.	Western suit

妈　妈：你看这套怎么样？这是去年春节买的，你一直没舍得穿，
　　　　叫什么拉的名牌。

翎　子：是"尼诺里拉"。

妈　妈：我没你脑子好使，记不住那么多牌儿，不过这料子确实
　　　　真好。

爸　爸：行，就是它了[N8]。给我找一条红色的领带。

妈　妈：咱们家没有红的，这个就差不多，给你吧。

爸　爸：成。

翎　子：不行，不行，鲜亮的领带怎么可以配正装西服呢？得，还
　　　　是我去帮你找一条合适的吧。

妈　妈：哎，这个还要吗？

爸　爸：当然留着了，好，这是正统货的标志，说不定还是老外的
　　　　"国货"呢，这对我太有利了。

17.	春节	Chūn Jié	N.	Spring Festival; Chinese New Year
18.	舍得	shěde	v.	willing to part with; not grudge
19.	名牌	míngpái	n.	brand name
20.	尼诺里拉	Nínuòlǐlā	N.	Ninoriva (an Italian brand)
21.	好使	hǎoshǐ	adj.	effective
22.	牌儿	páir	n.	brand (colloq.)
23.	料子	liàozi	n.	fabric
24.	领带	lǐngdài	n.	necktie; tie
25.	鲜亮	xiānliàng	adj.	bright and glossy
26.	正装	zhèngzhuāng	n.	formal suit
27.	西服	xīfú	n.	西装, Western suit
28.	正统	zhèngtǒng	adj.	authentic
29.	标志	biāozhì	n.	sign; mark
30.	说不定	shuōbudìng	v.	perhaps; maybe
31.	国货	guóhuò	n.	product of one's own country
32.	有利	yǒulì	adj.	advantageous; beneficial

翎　子：老爸，这商标可要剪了。

妈　妈：这可是外国的名牌标志，你爸还得**指着**[N9]它跟别人**套近乎**哪！

翎　子：还[N10]**套近乎**呢，不被人家笑话就不错了。你看人家外国**元首**们**会面**，一[N11]**屋子**人都穿名牌西服，有哪个留着商标的？快**剪**了吧。

爸　爸：怎么样？

妈　妈：哟，不错！

翎　子：帅！呀，老爸，这**扣子**不能**扣**的，这叫**风度扣**，是**装饰品**，不能**扣**。

爸　爸：**风度扣**？这老外就是**鬼点子**多，还"风度扣"……

翎　子：爸，这是人家的**着装**习惯。既然您穿西装**出席正式**场合，

33.	老爸	lǎobà	n.	(a colloquial form of address for father)
34.	商标	shāngbiāo	n.	trademark; brand mark
35.	剪	jiǎn	v.	cut (with scissors)
36.	指着	zhǐzhe	v.	(see note 9)
37.	套近乎	tào jìnhu	vo.	make friends; chum up
38.	元首	yuánshǒu	n.	head of state
39.	会面	huì miàn	vo.	meet
40.	一屋子	yì wūzi		a roomful of
41.	扣子	kòuzi	n.	button
42.	扣	kòu	v.	button up
43.	风度	fēngdù	n.	posture; bearing
44.	风度扣	fēngdùkòu	n.	decorative button on a jacket
45.	装饰品	zhuāngshìpǐn	n.	ornament; decoration
46.	鬼点子	guǐdiǎnzi	n.	tricky ideas
47.	着装	zhuózhuāng	n.	dressing
48.	出席	chūxí	v.	attend
49.	正式	zhèngshì	adj.	formal; official

就要了解穿西装的讲究，这是对人家尊重的表示。你可千万不要露怯呀！

爸　爸：是是是，还是咱们家小礼仪老师说得对。

翎　子：走啊！

爸　爸：干吗去呀？

翎　子：吃西餐啊。

翎　子：爸，今天您的**招待**活动做得怎么样啊？让您注意的您都注意了吗？

爸　爸：注意啦。今儿那外国人特别高兴。下午让小刘陪他们**逛街**，还专门给我买礼物了呢！

翎　子：礼物，什么礼物？

爸　爸：在我包里呢，一双袜子。

翎　子：袜子？

翎　子：呀，爸，你怎么穿白色袜子呢。

爸　爸：哎，白袜子怎么了？

| 50. | 招待 | zhāodài | v. | receive; welcome |
| 51. | 逛街 | guàng jiē | vo. | go sightseeing on streets; go window-shopping |

翎　子：您知道穿西服是不能穿白色袜子的！

爸　爸：为什么呀？

翎　子：为什么？

翎　子：别看穿衣戴帽这些小事情，不注意的话可是要**闹大笑话**的。

爸　爸：你这么一说倒**提醒**我了，咱们的小礼仪老师，能不能给我们的员工**培训**一下？

翎　子：行，没问题，包在我身上。

爸　爸：**一言为定**？

翎　子：一言为定！

爸　爸：好。

52.	闹(大)笑话	nào (dà) xiàohua	vo.	become the laughing stock; make a fool of oneself
53.	提醒	tíxǐng	v.	remind
54.	培训	péixùn	v.	train; training
55.	一言为定	yì yán wéi dìng		it's a deal; that's settled

注释　Notes

1. **"美姿美仪"**:

    这里指人的姿态、仪表美。

    The term refers to the grace of a person's bearing and appearance.

2. **"说起来……"**:

    Speaking of...

    在提起一件事或一个人时，可以用"说起来……"，也可以说"说起……（来）"。

    When someone or something is mentioned in the conversation and subsequently becomes the new topic, the structure "说起来……" can be used.

    (1) 说起来臭美，我倒想起来了……

    Speaking of being showy, it just made me think of...

    (2) 说起校长来，老师们都有说不完的话。

    When it comes to the principal, the teachers all have a lot to say.

    (3) 说起手机来，我问你，你看见我的手机了吗？

    Speaking of cell phones, I have to ask you, did you see my cell phone?

3. **"穿得出去"**:

    "穿得出去"的意思是：一件衣服可以穿上出现在别人面前或公众场合，而不会引起别人笑话或耻笑。

    This colloquial expression pertains to the quality and grade of clothes. It means (the clothes are) decent enough for one to wear and to go out in without feeling embarrassed.

    (1) 给我找一身穿得出去的行头，明天我要跟外宾谈判。

    Find me a decent suit. I have a meeting with some foreigners tomorrow.

    (2) 这条裙子太短了，我这么大年纪，怎么穿得出去？

    This skirt is too short. How can someone of my age go out wearing something like that?

    (3) 这种衣服太便宜了，正式晚会穿不出去。

    This kind of clothes is too cheap, and inappropriate for formal parties.

4. "省得":

意思是：（做什么）使不好的事情不会发生，意思同"避免"。口语。

This colloquial term is used in a sense pretty close to that of the English "lest", but more informal.

(1) 我是说这里边有什么讲究没有，省得我明天跟人吃饭时露怯。

What I tried to ask is whether there is anything particular about it, so that I will not cut a poor figure when I go to dinner with others tomorrow.

(2) 你别来了，我上班正好从你那里过，我给你送去吧，省得你跑一趟。

You don't have to come. I can bring it to you on my way to work, to save you a trip.

(3) 这件事你别告诉爸爸，省得他又说我浪费。

Don't tell my dad about it, otherwise he will again scold me for being wasteful.

5. "露怯":

"露怯"的意思是：因为缺乏某种知识，在说话或者动作行为方面出现了可笑的错误。口语。

This slang term means "to make a show of oneself" or "to become a laughing stock" because of one's ignorance of social manners.

(1) 我是说这里边有什么讲究没有，省得我明天跟人吃饭时露怯。

What I tried to ask is whether there is anything particular about it, so that I will not cut a poor figure when I go to dinner with others tomorrow.

(2) 别露怯了，吃西餐得右手用刀，左手用叉子。

Don't make a fool of yourself: Eating a Western meal, you should hold the knife in your right hand and the folk in your left hand.

(3) 你又露怯了。吃烤鸭，酱要放在饼里边，不能像你这样沾着吃。

You're playing the fool again. To eat roast duck, the sauce is to be put in the wrap. Don't dip the wrap into the sauce as you did.

6. "黑":

"黑"的意思是"狠毒"、"坏"。用于商人时，指他们商品的要价太高或欺骗顾客。口语。

In a colloquial usage, "黑" means "wicked" or "sinister". When it pertains to a businessman, it typically refers to his practice of setting exorbitant prices and deceiving the customers.

(1) 这孩子还真有经济头脑啊，说吧，多少钱？别太黑喽。

This child really has a head for economics! Tell me, how much do you want? But don't be too greedy.

(2) 这个饭馆儿真黑，菜太贵了，量又少。

That restaurant ['s owner] is really avaricious. The food is so expensive and portion is too small.

(3) 那个老板很黑，你要小心别上当。

That shopkeeper is truly a wicked person. Don't let yourself be fooled by him!

7. "边……边……":

意思和"一边……一边……"一样。

This is a more informal form of "一边……一边……".

(1) 边实践边学习，行。

Learning while practicing—that's fine.

(2) 咱们边吃边谈吧。

Let's have a chat while eating.

(3) 我上课的时候不习惯边听老师讲课边记笔记。

I am not used to taking notes while listening to the professor in class.

8. "就是它了":

This is it.

选中某物或某人时，可以这样说。

It is an expression to be used when a selection is determined.

(1) 妈妈：你看这套怎么样？这是去年春节买的。

Mother: How do you like this suit? It was bought around the Spring Festival last year.

爸爸：行，就是它了。

Father: Fine. This is it.

(2) A：这三个人谁跟你一起去好？

Who among the three do you want to go with you?

B：三个人都不错，嗯，就是这个高个子了。

All three are pretty good. Hmmm, this tall guy will be the one.

9. "指着":

意思是：依靠（人或物）。口语。

"指着", as a colloquialism, means "to count on" or "to depend on".

(1) 你老爸还指着它和别人套近乎呢。

Your dad was counting on it to chum up with others.

(2) 儿子，我还指着你养活我呢。

Son, I count on you for support.

(3) 我就指着这台电脑挣钱吃饭呢。你给我弄丢了，怎么办？

I wholly relied on that computer for making a living, and you lost it. What shall I do?

10. 副词"还"（二）：

见第六课《还得学》注释4。

For the use of the adverb "还", see note 4 in Lesson 6.

11. "一"：

"一"在一些名词充当的临时名量词前可以表示"满"的意思。比如"一屋子人"、"一头汗"、"一手泥"、"一身土"、"一口上海话"等。

Used before a noun, the numeral "一" becomes close to the adjective "满" (full) in meaning, e. g.："一屋子人"(a houseful of people), "一头汗"(with one's head covered with sweat), "一手泥"(with the hand covered by mud), "一身土"(with dust all over), "一口上海话"(speaking unadulterated Shanghainese), etc.

听说练习　Listening & Speaking Exercises

■ 一、课文理解 Text Comprehension

（一）根据故事情节选择适当的答案

Please choose the most appropriate answer based on the story

1. 翎子是做什么工作的？（　　）
   A. 谈判　　　　　　B. 演戏　　　　　　C. 外事服务

2. 爸爸到家的时候，妈妈和女儿在做什么呢？（　　）
   A. 女儿教妈妈走路　　B. 女儿教妈妈美姿美仪　　C. 女儿教妈妈演戏

3. 爸爸觉得太太（　　）
   A. 爱演戏　　　　　　B. 挺美的　　　　　　C. 爱臭美

4. 爸爸为什么要妈妈给他找一身穿得出去的行头？（　　）
   A. 明天要跟外宾谈判　　B. 明天要学外事服务　　C. 明天要请教问题

5. 爸爸要请教女儿一些问题，因为他怕（　　）
   A. 露怯　　　　　　B. 穿西装　　　　　　C. 吃西餐

6. 爸爸为什么要留着西装上的商标？（　　）
   A. 他认为对他谈判有利
   B. 他认为是老外的"国货"
   C. 他认为是正统货的标志

7. 在翎子看来，鲜亮的领带配正装西服非常（　　）
   A. 好看　　　　　　B. 合适　　　　　　C. 不合适

8. 翎子说穿衣戴帽这种小事情不注意的话会闹（　　）
   A. 笑话　　　　　　B. 肚子　　　　　　C. 袜子

（二）根据课文判断下面句子意思的正误

State whether the following statements are true or false based on the story

1. （　　）女儿爱臭美，爸爸非常讨厌。

2.（   ）爸爸认为太太比女儿好看。

3.（   ）翎子很有经济头脑，爸爸不花钱她是不会帮助他的。

4.（   ）爸爸很喜欢那套"尼诺里拉"西装，常常穿着去上班。

5.（   ）翎子告诉爸爸鲜亮的领带配正装西服不合适。

6.（   ）爸爸不想剪掉西装上的商标是想指着它和外国人套近乎。

7.（   ）爸爸不喜欢外国人，认为老外就是鬼点子多。

8.（   ）翎子爸爸今天见外国人没有露怯。

（三）先听故事叙述，然后复述故事

Listen to the narrative first and then retell the story

翎子是学外事服务的。爸爸今天请教女儿几个关于穿衣服的问题，因为明天要跟外宾谈判，怕露怯。女儿开玩笑说，他得"交学费"，请她和她妈妈去吃西餐。

爸爸让妈妈给他找一套合适的西装，妈妈就把去年春节买的一套名牌西装拿来。爸爸想配一条红领带，翎子说鲜亮的领带配正装西服不合适。爸爸想留着西服上的商标，这样别人可以知道他穿的是正统货，翎子说这样会被别人笑话。翎子还详细地告诉爸爸哪个扣子能扣，哪个扣子不能扣。

第二天爸爸下班回来以后告诉翎子，今天的接待活动很好，外国人都特别高兴，还专门给他买了一双袜子作为礼物。翎子这时才知道爸爸今天还是露怯了。

■ 二、词语使用 Application of Vocabulary and Grammar

（一）选择题

Choose the item that is grammatically correct

1. 你妈平时就_____美的，倒是你呀，太爱臭美了。

　　A. 挺　　　　B. 常　　　　C. 是　　　　D. 爱

2. 说_____臭美，我倒想起来了。翎子妈，我的西服呢？

　　A. 起来　　　B. 看来　　　C. 上来　　　D. 出来

3. 给我找一_____穿得出去的行头，明天我要跟外宾谈判。

　　A. 件　　　　B. 条　　　　C. 身　　　　D. 双

4. 有问题请教？说吧，是不是_____臭美的问题呀？

　　A. 问到　　　B. 关于　　　C. 请教　　　D. 对于

5. 我是说吃西餐这里边有 _____ 讲究没有，省得我明天跟人吃饭时露怯。

    A. 什么   B. 一种   C. 很多   D. 哪些

6. 讲究当然有啦，可我也不能 _____ 教您啊，是不是？您要交点儿学费。

    A. 专   B. 喜欢   C. 黑   D. 白

7. 你看这套怎么样？这是去年春节买的，你 _____ 没舍得穿，是名牌的。

    A. 好的   B. 新的   C. 一直   D. 一来

8. 还和外国人套近乎呢，不被人家笑话 _____ 不错了。

    A. 很   B. 就   C. 才   D. 是

（二）选择题

Circle the answer that best reflects the meaning of the underlined portion of the sentence

1. 给我找一身穿得出去的行头，明天我要跟外宾谈判。（   ）

    A. 出门穿的

    B. 穿出去合适

    C. 穿着舒服

    D. 大小合适

2. 这件事你别告诉爸爸，省得他又说我浪费。（   ）

    A. 节省   B. 得省

    C. 恐怕   D. 避免

3. 讲究当然有啦，可我也不能白教您啊。（   ）

    A. 白天教

    B. 晚上教

    C. 不收钱教

    D. 我付钱教

4. 这孩子还真有经济头脑啊，说吧，多少钱？别太黑喽。（   ）

    A. 让我害怕

    B. 要价太高

    C. 良心不好

    D. 没有良心

5. 你看这套"尼诺里拉"怎么样？这是去年春节买的，你一直<u>没舍得穿</u>。

（　　）

A. 没地方穿

B. 没机会穿

C. 舍不得穿

D. 没宿舍穿

（三）选择适当的词语，替换句中的画线部分

Choose the most appropriate words to replace the underlined parts

A. 露怯	B. 指着	C. 讲究
D. 说起 N 来	E. 说不定	F. 套近乎

1. 吃西餐有什么特别<u>值得注意</u>的事情没有？

2. 你又<u>闹笑话</u>了。吃烤鸭，酱要放在饼里边，不能像你这样沾着吃。

3. <u>提到</u>手机，我问你，你看见我的手机了吗？

4. 很多中国人老了以后<u>依靠</u>儿子养活。

5. 这商标是正统货的标志，<u>可能</u>还是老外的"国货"呢。

6. 可不是吗，你爸还得指着它和别人<u>拉关系</u>哪！

（四）用所给词语完成对话

Complete the following dialogues with the items provided in the parenthesis

1. （指着，就是它了）

爸爸：翎子妈，给我找一身穿得出去的行头，明天我要跟外宾谈判。

妈妈：你看这套怎么样？这是去年春节买的。

爸爸：行，_____。

妈妈：我说翎子他爸，你也不能老_____我照顾你。以后穿什么你自己找吧！

2. （有什么讲究，专门，白，一言为定）

陈燕：我们公司很多人对吃西餐、穿西服到底_____还真不清楚。

翎子：我是_____学外事服务的，可以去你们公司给你们上一课。

陈燕：那太好了，这个周末行吗？

翎子：可我不能_____教啊！

陈燕：一小时二百元，你看怎么样？

翎子：好，_____。

3. （说不定，说起……来，边……边……）

妈妈：这老外也真有意思，还送给你个礼物。

爸爸：_____礼物_____，我还在琢磨，他们为什么送我一双袜子呢？

妈妈：_____是因为他们看你穿着一双白袜子，以为你没有买黑袜子的钱了。

爸爸：看来，我还得_____实践_____学习呀！

妈妈：我跟你逗着玩儿呢，翎子爸！

（五）角色扮演 Role play

Make a dialogue with a classmate. One party plays Lingzi, and the other plays her father. Your dialogue should incorporate the provided items.

爸爸	翎子
You are not a man who would usually fuss over clothing and manners; hence, you often make fun of your daughter for paying too much attention to people's appearances since her profession is "social etiquette". Today just after you told her off again for being showy then you realized that you will have a negotiation meeting with some foreign guests tomorrow. You don't want to act or look awkward for this occasion. You need your daughter's expertise now. Though your daughter is more than happy to help, she realizes this is a rare opportunity to get back at you. She asks for a fee for her lesson. You happily settle on a price for your education.	"Social etiquette" is your profession. Your father has just told you off again, in an affectionate way, for being showy when he realized that he will have a negotiation meeting with some foreign guests tomorrow. Your father tells you that he has a question that needs your attention. Using the opportunity to get back at him, you ask him whether his question has something to do with being "showy"? For all his "criticisms", he does not want to look awkward for this occasion. Hence, he needs your expertise on how to eat a western-style meal and what is proper to wear. Claiming that you can't teach him for nothing, you cheekily ask him for a tuition payment. A dinner in a Western-style restaurant is happily agreed upon as the payment.

1. 跟外宾谈判	2. 外事服务	1. 臭美的问题	2. 用嘴吃
3. 请教	4. 西餐	3. 当然有啦	4. 不能白教
5. 讲究	6. 省得	5. 至于	6. 学费
7. 露怯	8. 经济头脑	7. 西餐厅	8. 吃顿西餐
9. 别太黑喽			
10. 边实践边学习			

■ 三、课堂讨论 Discussion

1. 翎子和爸爸的关系怎么样？请举例说明。

2. 外国朋友为什么给爸爸买了一双袜子作为礼物？

3. 爸爸为什么要翎子培训公司的员工？

4. 中国人说"入乡随俗"，英文有"When in Rome do as the Romans do"，谈谈你对这种说法的看法。

第二十课 改 口

Clean up Your Act

编剧：许长宝　翟顺元

人物（Characters）

许老爷子（Xǔ lǎoyézi）——男，六十岁左右。

佟大妈（Tóng dàmā）——女，五十五岁左右，许大爷的老伴。

许刚（Xǔ Gāng）——男，三十岁左右，许大爷的儿子。

强子（Qiángzi）——男，三十岁左右，许刚的**好友**。

四五个老爷子（sìwǔ gè lǎoyézi）

一个小孩儿（yí gè xiǎoháir）

一对男女老外（yí duì nánnǚ lǎowài）

---

1. 改口	gǎi kǒu	vo.	(see note 1)
2. 大妈	dàmā	n.	aunt（an affectionate or respectful form of address for an elderly woman）; father's elder brother's wife
3. 好友	hǎo yǒu		good friend
4. 小孩儿	xiǎoháir	n.	child; kid
5. 老外	lǎowài	n.	foreigner

课 文 Text

许老爷子：哟呵，**各位**，**早班**[N2]早班。

甲老爷子：**少见啊**！

许老爷子：哟呵，各位，都来了啊！

甲老爷子：我说老哥哥，这些日子没见，哪儿看**西洋景**[N3]去了？

许老爷子：看西洋景就好喽，给闺女呀当**保姆**去啦，告诉我三四天，我也没带**鸟**啊，好，**溜溜**俩多**礼拜**[N4]啊。哎，我不在你们都**拔了份**[N5]了吧。

鸟 叫 声：**臭脚**！换人！臭脚！换人！傻……

丙老爷子：哎哟喂[N6]，这鸟儿怎么脏了口[N7]了这鸟？

乙老爷子：可不是吗，走走走走走，咱们回家！

小 孙 子：爷爷，爷爷，再玩儿会儿嘛！这么多小鸟在唱歌多好听啊！

乙老爷子：好听？再待会儿啊，咱们这鸟就跟那**骂人**的鸟学坏喽！

---

6. 各位	gè wèi		everybody; you-all
7. 早班	zǎo bān		(see note 2)
8. 少见	shǎo jiàn	v.	haven't seen you for a while; long time no see
9. 西洋景	xīyángjǐng	n.	(see note 3)
10. 保姆	bǎomǔ	n.	nanny; housekeeper
11. 鸟	niǎo	n.	bird
12. 溜溜	liūliū	adv.	(see note 4)
13. 礼拜	lǐbài	n.	week
14. 拔（了）份	bá (le) fèn	vo.	(see note 5)
15. 臭	chòu	adj.	(of smell) stinky; smelly
16. 孙子	sūnzi	n.	grandson
17. 骂人	mà rén	vo.	swear (at people)

许老爷子：各位，别价！都别动，我**撤**……

甲老爷子：多好的鸟啊，完喽……

.

许老爷子：大刚！……大刚！

佟 大 妈：大刚去给你买**鸟食**去了。

许老爷子：买鸟食？我用不着，就是他，我这脸都丢**尽**了……

佟 大 妈：哎哟，这大刚怎么又**招**你了？你那个鸟还不全靠大刚啊。

许老爷子：靠他？要不靠他啊——我这鸟还**不至于脏口**了呢！

佟 大 妈：脏口？……

许老爷子：刚子！**站住**！

许　　刚：爸，怎么了？吓我一跳。

许老爷子：我问你，这鸟怎么回事儿啊？怎么脏口了？

许　　刚：脏口了？

许老爷子：一会儿一个[N8]"臭脚、臭脚"，一会儿一个"换人、换人"！

许　　刚：爸，这不算什么**脏话**吧这个？

18. 撤	chè	v.	withdraw; go back
19. 鸟食	niǎo shí	n.	food for birds
20. 尽	jìn	adv.	completely
21. 招	zhāo	v.	provoke
22. 不至于	bú zhìyú		cannot go so far; be unlikely
23. 脏口	zāng kǒu	vo.	have a foul mouth
24. 站住	zhàn zhù	vc.	stop; halt
25. 脏话	zānghuà	n.	obscene; dirty or foul language

许老爷子：**不止**这些呢，你听一会儿一个傻……我都**没法说**呀，就
是你们老说的那个……

许　　刚：不是，爸，不会吧，我可没给它教这个，不信你问强子？

强　　子：这您是真错怪许刚了，就为您这鸟，他可真没少**下工夫**，
您瞧，这**面包虫**我们刚从**官园**买回来的。

佟　大　妈：哎呀，我说老头子，你还有完没完了[N9]？来来，你们俩
进来进来，甭**搭理**他，过来过来过来。

许　　刚：**长出息**了你[N10]，你说我**冤**不冤？

26.	不止	bùzhǐ	v.	more than; not limited to
27.	没法说	méi fǎ shuō		can't describe
28.	下工夫	xià gōngfu	vo.	make efforts; work hard
29.	面包虫	miànbāochóng	n.	(a kind of insect)
30.	官园	Guānyuán	N.	(name of a market)
31.	搭理	dāli	v.	(usu. used in the negative) respond; answer
32.	长出息	zhǎng chūxi	vo.	become more capable
33.	冤	yuān	adj.	be wronged; be treated unfairly

强　　子：你爸是不（是）**搞错**了？

许　　刚：怎么可能呢……光**顾**着跟老爷子**咋呼**[N11]了，今儿还有球赛呢。

强　　子：北京**国安**对上海。

（电视：假**动作晃动**，**连续**两个假动作，又**晃**过……）

许　　刚：踢呀……

（电视：臭脚、臭脚……换人、换人……傻……）

（一个月以后……）

鸟　　儿：欢迎，欢迎。

女 老 外：Hello!（你好！）

鸟　　儿：How do you do?（你好吗？）

女 老 外：It can speak English!（它能说英语！）That's great!（太棒了！）

许老爷子：这口儿啊是我儿子教的。

女 老 外：Your bird is beautiful!（你的鸟好漂亮！）

男 老 外：Beijing is wonderful!（北京，真棒！）

34.	搞错	gǎo cuò	vc.	make a mistake
35.	顾	gù	v.	pay attention to
36.	咋呼	zhāhu	v.	talk; argue (as used in this story)
37.	国安	Guó'ān	N.	(name of a football team)
38.	动作	dòngzuò	n.	movement; motion; action
39.	晃动	huǎngdòng	v.	rock; sway
40.	连续	liánxù	v.	successive; continuous
41.	晃	huǎng	v.	sway

许老爷子：我就**不信这个邪**[N12]，就这么个小**玩意**儿，愣**哨**出脏口，
我能**扳不过来**[N13]？**姥姥**[N14]！

丙老爷子：要**搁**[N15]着过去啊，这个鸟一脏了口就得**摔**死它，要想重
新**押口**[N16]，难了……

乙老爷子：**依我看**啊，咱们语言中的脏话，也要改改口儿，**免得**[N17]
外人笑话啊，你说是不是？

许老爷子：对，没错，甭管是北京的鸟还是北京的人，谁要**出了脏
口**，咱们也得把他给扳过来。

42. 不信(这个)邪	bú xìn (zhè ge) xié		(see note 12)
43. 玩意儿	wányìr	n.	a little thing; toy
44. 哨	shào	v.	chirp; utter sound(by a bird)
45. 扳	bān	v.	correct
46. 姥姥	lǎolao		(see note 14)
47. 搁着过去	gēzhe guòqù		in the past(colloq.)
48. 摔	shuāi	v.	cause to fall and break; knock
49. 重新	chóngxīn	adv.	once again; once more
50. 押口	yā kǒu	vo.	(see note 16)
51. 依我看	yī wǒ kàn		in my opinion
52. 免得	miǎnde	conj.	so as not to; so as to avoid
53. 出(了)脏口	chū (le) zāngkǒu	vo.	speak dirty words; have a foul mouth

1. **"改口"**:

　　本课"改口"的意思是改变鸟的"脏口"。

　　"改口" in this lesson refers to changing the parrot's habit of uttering dirty words.

2. **"早班"**:

　　"早班"本来的意思是指工作中按照上班的时间分为早班、中班、晚班。本剧中的"早班早班"用于打招呼，意思是：你们来得早，你们来得早。口语。

　　"早班" is usually used to refer to the "morning shift" as opposed to normal shift or night shift. However，"早班" in this lesson is used in greeting：You guys are early today.

3. **"西洋景"**:

　　是过去民间的一种娱乐设备，也叫拉洋片，因为当时其中出现的画面都是西方的画。本剧的"哪儿看西洋景去了"是问"去哪儿玩儿（比如旅游）了"。口语。

　　"西洋景" is used to refer to a kind of traditional folk entertainment. It is also called "拉洋片"（"foreign slide show"）because all the slides show foreign scenes. "西洋景" in these days is used to refer to rare scenes. By "哪儿看西洋景去了?" the speaker is asking "Where have you traveled?"

4. **"溜溜俩多礼拜"**:

　　"溜溜"在这里表示说话人觉得时间长。"俩"的意思是"两个"，注意后边不能再用量词。都是口语。

　　"溜溜"，a colloquial expression，is used to refer to a lengthy time span. Note a measure word cannot co-occur with "俩"，which means "两个".

5. **"拔份"**:

　　意思是：出风头。方言。

　　"拔份" is used in Northern dialect，and means "to seek the limelight".

6. **"哎哟喂"**:

表示惊讶、意外。

An interjection similar to "Wow!" or "Goodness!"

7. **"脏口"**:

指画眉、百灵等叫声好听的鸟，叫出不好听的声音，比如学乌鸦叫；也指鹦鹉、八哥等会学人说话的鸟说了脏话、骂人的坏话。

"脏口" refers to birds，such as thrushes or larks，that usually chirp make unpleasant sounds like crow's cry. In this lesson，however，it refers to those parrots uttering dirty words.

8. **"一会儿一个"**:

意思是：很频繁地做什么。"Frequently" or "every so often" "一会儿一个 '臭脚、臭脚'，一会儿一个 '换人、换人'"，意思是说那个鸟常常说 "臭脚" 和 "换人"。

This sentence means that the bird frequently says "臭脚" or "换人".

9. **"你还有完没完了"**:

这是反问句。这里的意思是：你不应该再说了。

This is a rhetorical question that means "Are you finished yet?" By saying it，the speaker means to say "be quiet".

10. **"长出息了你"**:

这是一种倒装句。见第二课注释2。

"You've grown up，haven't you?"，this is an inverted sentence. Please see note 2 of Lesson 2.

11. **"咋呼"**:

这里的意思是：大声地、没有顾忌地说话。北方方言。

"咋呼'，an expression in Northern dialect，meaning to speak aloud without any consideration of others.

(1) 光顾着跟老爷子咋呼了，今儿还有球赛呢。

I've been chatting with the old man for so long and almost forgot today's ball game.

(2) 大家都睡觉了，你别在这儿咋呼了。

Everybody is in bed now. Don't be so talkative here.

(3) 你说这些，是瞎咋呼，没用！

What you said was nothing but bluff talk. It was useless.

12. "我就不信这个邪"：

当相信遇到的困难或挑战是可以克服、战胜的时，说话人可以这样说，表示自己的信心。

"I just won't believe it!", this is often said when one encounters difficulties or challenges to show one's determination.

13. "扳不过来"：

"扳"的本来意思是"使位置固定的东西改变方向或转动"。"我就不信这个邪，就这么个小玩意儿，愣哨出脏口儿，我能扳不过来?"这句话中，"扳"的意思是"使改变"。上面这个句子的意思是：我不信，就这么一个小鸟，偏偏"说"出脏话，我还不能叫它改过来?

"扳" literally means "to change the direction of a fixed object, or to change someone's bad habit". In this lesson, the speaker is saying that "I just don't believe that I cannot change a small bird that 'speaks' dirty words."

14. 姥姥：

也写作"老老"，据考来自满族语，表示对某人某事不服气或轻蔑的语气，可用于反驳、争吵。本剧中许老爷子针对的可能是那只鸟和其他养鸟人。

"姥姥"也写作"老老" is used to express a contemptuous and scornful sentiment towards someone or something during an argument. This expression originated possibly from the Manchu dialect. "姥姥" used here by 许老爷子 indicates that he scorns such an assumption by other bird keepers that this foul—mouthed bird can not be changed.

15. "搁（要搁着过去啊）"：

"搁"这里是"放（在）"的意思。口语。

"搁" means "to place". "要搁着过去", a colloquial term often used in Northern dialect, meaning "if in the past, …".

16. "押口"：

训练鸟学各种声音。To train a bird to imitate all sounds.

17. "免得"：

意思基本同"省得"。参见第十九课注释 4。"省得"更加口语。

"免得" is similar to the meaning of "省得" ("so as not to", or "to avoid"), except that "省得" is more colloquial than "免得". Please refer to note 4 of Lesson 19.

（1）依我看啊，咱们语言中的脏话，也要改改口，免得外人笑话啊，你说是不是？

I think we need to stop using dirty words as well so that we won't be laughted at by others. Don't you think so?

（2）把剩下的菜打包带回家吧，免得浪费。

Let's take home the leftovers so that we don't waste it.

（3）你快把书给他送去吧，免得他着急。

You need to hurry and send the book to him. Otherwise, he will get anxious.

听说练习　Listening & Speaking Exercises

一、课文理解 Text Comprehension

（一）根据故事情节选择适当的答案

Please choose the most appropriate answer based on the story

1. 许老爷子来公园是为了（　　）

    A. 见朋友　　　　　　B. 走路　　　　　　C. 遛鸟

2. 许老爷子前两个星期（　　）

    A. 去女儿家了　　　　B. 去看西洋景了　　C. 去遛鸟了

3. 现在许老爷子的鸟会（　　）

    A. 说话了　　　　　　B. 骂人了　　　　　C. 唱歌了

4. 别的老人要离开，因为（　　）

    A. 他们的鸟比不上许老爷子的鸟

    B. 他们不喜欢许老爷子

    C. 他们怕他们的鸟跟许老爷子的鸟学坏

5. 许老爷子很生他儿子的气，因为他觉得儿子（　　）

    A. 不给鸟买鸟食　　　B. 不去遛鸟　　　　C. 教鸟骂人

6. 许老爷子的儿子喜欢（　　）

    A. 打球　　　　　　　B. 看球赛　　　　　C. 看电影

7. 教鸟学坏的是（　　）

    A. 电视　　　　　　　B. 别的鸟　　　　　C. 许老爷子的儿子

8. 一个月以后，许老爷子把鸟（　　）

    A. 给儿子了　　　　　B. 扳过来了　　　　C. 摔死了

（二）根据课文判断下面句子意思的正误

State whether the following statements are true or false based on the story

1. （　　）许老爷子认识公园里其他的老爷子。

2. （　　）许老爷子在女儿家住了三四天。

3. （　　）以前许老爷子的鸟比其他人的鸟差。

4. （　　）其他的老爷子都不喜欢许老爷子的鸟说脏话。

5. （　　）许老爷子的儿子教鸟说脏话。

6. （　　）许老爷子不许他的鸟说脏话。

7. （　　）许老爷子教他的鸟说英语。

（三）先听故事叙述，然后复述故事

Listen to the narrative first and then retell the story

　　许老爷子去女儿家住了两个星期，回来以后发现他的鸟学会说脏话了。其他的养鸟人都不愿意跟他在一起，怕自己的鸟也学坏了。许老爷子气死了，因为他从来都没有这么丢人现眼过。他想，这鸟儿是跟谁学的呢？这些脏话都是球迷们常说的。对了，儿子是个球迷，看球的时候肯定说了脏话，……

　　可是许老爷子问儿子的时候，儿子说他从来不说脏话。那是谁的错呢？正在这时候，儿子打开电视看球赛，许老爷子听到电视里看球赛的人大喊大叫的声音，才知道，他错怪儿子了。

　　后来许老爷子的儿子教鸟说英语，那只鸟再也不说脏话了。

二、词语使用 Application of Vocabulary and Grammar

（一）选择题

Choose the item that is grammatically correct

1. 真有意思，你这只小鸟会说英语，＿＿＿＿＿＿谁学的？

　　A. 招　　　　　B. 靠　　　　　C. 从　　　　　D. 跟

2. A：现在一张球赛票可贵了，差不多二百块钱。

　　B：＿＿＿＿＿＿二百块钱，听说五百呢！

　　A. 没错　　　　B. 不止　　　　C. 多　　　　　D. 连

3. 昨天的篮球赛是中国队＿＿＿＿＿＿日本队。中国队赢了。

　　A. 对　　　　　B. 跟　　　　　C. 和　　　　　D. 都

4. 我的朋友对中文很有兴趣，为了写好汉字，他可真＿＿＿＿＿＿。

　　A. 不至于　　　B. 没完没了　　C. 没少下工夫　　D. 太棒了

5. 你最好给妈妈打一个电话，告诉她你今天会晚一点儿回家，

　　＿＿＿＿＿＿她不放心。

A. 不至于　　　　B. 免得　　　　C. 用不着　　　　D. 吓一跳

（二）选择题

Circle the answer that best reflects the meaning of the sentence

1. 各位，早班早班。（　　　）

   A. 大家都上早班

   B. 大家都起得比我早

   C. 大家都来得很早

   D. 大家都早上上班

2. 这些日子没见，哪儿看西洋景去了？（　　　）

   A. 这些天没见面，去哪儿玩儿了？

   B. 这些天没见面，去西洋景了吗？

   C. 这些天没见面，哪儿有西洋景？

   D. 这些天没见面，去西洋看景了吗？

3. 看西洋景就好了，给闺女当保姆去啦。（　　　）

   A. 女儿去看西洋景了，所以我得帮女儿带孩子。

   B. 看西洋景不错，可是我得帮女儿带孩子。

   C. 西洋景很好看，我跟女儿和保姆一起去啦。

   D. 我哪有福气去玩儿啊，我去女儿家帮她带孩子去了。

4. 要不靠他啊——我这鸟还不至于脏口了呢！（　　　）

   A. 我的鸟没学说脏话，多亏了他。

   B. 我的鸟学会说脏话了，我得去找他。

   C. 就是因为他帮忙，我的鸟才学会说脏话了。

   D. 我的鸟学会说脏话了，我得靠他帮助扳过来。

5. 就为这鸟，他可真没少下工夫。（　　　）

   A. 为了养好这只鸟，他花了很多时间，做了很多事。

   B. 为了养好这只鸟，他花了很多钱。

   C. 为了养好这只鸟，他没花时间。

   D. 为了养好这只鸟，他每天去买鸟食。

6. 就是他，今天我这脸都丢尽了。（　　　）

   A. 我有他这样的儿子真觉得丢脸。

   B. 我为了他觉得很丢脸。

   C. 他今天让我真丢脸了。

D. 就是因为他，我今天真丢脸了，脸都丢光了。

(三) 选择适当的词语，替换句中的画线部分

Choose the most appropriate words to replace the underlined parts

| A. 要搁着过去 | B. 用不着 | C. 没完 | D. 不信这个邪呢 |
| E. 不止这些 | F. 免得 | G. 不信 | |

1. 现在在中国上一个好大学，一年的学费差不多一万块钱，<u>以前</u>，一分钱都不用花。

2. 你还没有准备好行李吗？你去北京，<u>不用带这么多东西</u>，在那儿什么都买得到。<u>要是你不相信我的话</u>，你可以问我的同屋。

3. A：这课的功课就是练习二到练习五，对不对？

　B：<u>比这些多</u>，还有练习七和八呢！

4. A：听说这个教授的课非常难，上他的课，很难拿 A。

　B：<u>我才不相信这话呢</u>，我一定得上他的课，而且一定得拿 A！

5. 爸爸：我的日记本不见了，是不是圆圆拿错了？

　妈妈：你先问问她，<u>这样才不会冤枉她</u>。

6. A：我的女朋友什么都好，就是一说起话来，就<u>不停</u>。

　B：我的女朋友从来不多说话。

(四) 用所给词语完成对话

Complete the following dialogues with the items provided in the parenthesis

1. （吓我一跳，不至于）

　A：糟糕！我可能把电脑忘在图书馆了。

　B：你不是放在书架上了吗？

　A：哎哟，在这儿呢，＿＿＿＿＿＿＿＿。

　B：你的记性＿＿＿＿＿＿＿这么不好吧？

2. （不信，不止）

　A：后天我们要考的生词就是这三课里边的，对不对？

　B：＿＿＿＿＿＿＿这些，还有以前的生词。

　A：不会吧？

　B：＿＿＿＿＿＿＿你去问老师。

3. （用不着，免得）

　A：鸟食不够了，我去买点儿鸟食来吧。

　B：＿＿＿＿＿＿＿，厨房还有呢！

　A：那些不够。反正我还要买别的东西，现在买了，＿＿＿＿＿＿＿下个星期再去了。

4.（招，怎么可能，不信，错怪）

A：圆圆，你怎么这么不高兴？谁＿＿＿＿＿你了？

B：我爸爸的钱找不到了，说我拿了他的钱。

A：真的吗？＿＿＿＿＿呢？

B：是真的，＿＿＿＿＿你去问我妈妈！

A：他一定是＿＿＿＿＿你了。

（五）角色扮演 Role play

Make a dialogue with a classmate. One party plays old man Xu, and the other plays his son. Your dialogue should incorporate the provided items.

许老爷子	许刚
You are so happy to see your bird after two weeks' absence. When you take the bird to meet your friends as usual, your bird surprised you, and embarrasses you with dirty words. Who taught it? It must have been your son, who was taking care of the bird during your absence.	You cannot believe that your dad is so upset, because the bird speaks dirty words. No, you never taught him to do that! Your friend can prove it.
1. 怎么回事？ 2. 脸都丢尽了 3. 说脏话 4. 一会儿……一会儿……	1. 怎么了？吓我一跳！ 2. 我可没…… 3. 不信问…… 4. 错怪

■ 三、课堂讨论 Discussion

1. 许老爷子的鸟学会了说脏话，是谁的责任？

2. 许老爷子因为鸟说脏话觉得丢人现眼，是不是太认真了？

3. 你会不会因为你的宠物做了不好的事情觉得丢脸？

附录一：生词索引　Vocabulary Index

A

挨饿	ái è		be starved	6
癌症	áizhèng	n.	cancer	12
唉	ài	interj.	(model particle indicating a response)	1
碍	ài	v.	hinder; be in the way of	7
爱	ài	v.	like; be fond of	2
爱人	àiren	n.	spouse; husband or wife	14
爱心	àixīn	n.	love; compassion	10
案件	ànjiàn	n.	law suit; case	9
熬	áo	v.	endure; put up with	4
奥运会	Àoyùnhuì	N.	abbreviation of Olympic Games	6

B

巴不得	bābude	v.	cannot wait (to do sth.); be anxious (to do sth.)	8
拔（了）份	bá (le) fèn	vo.	(see note 5)	20
把握	bǎwò	n./v.	grasp; seize	7
白血病	báixuèbìng	n.	leukemia	12
摆	bǎi	v.	put; place	12
百姓	bǎixìng	n.	common people	1
扳	bān	v.	correct	20
搬弄是非	bānnòng shìfēi		(see note 14)	18
扳子	bānzi	n.	wrench	2
伴儿	bànr	n.	companion	12
办货	bàn huò	vo	purchase or buy goods wholesale	18
办事	bàn shì	vo.	handle affairs; do things	13
扮演	bànyǎn	v.	play the role of	17
榜样	bǎngyàng	n.	example; model	4
包	bāo	n.	bag	3
包括	bāokuò	v.	include	4
饱	bǎo	adj.	eat till full; full	6
保安	bǎo'ān	n.	security guard	13
宝贝	bǎobèi	n.	treasure	3

保不齐	bǎobuqí	adv.	(see note 15)	2
保姆	bǎomǔ	n.	nanny；housekeeper	20
保证	bǎozhèng	v.	guarantee；promise	4
曝光	bào guāng	vo.	expose (wrong doing in the newspaper or on TV)	16
爆炸性	bàozhàxìng	n.	explosive；unexpected	18
倍儿	bèir	adv.	extremely；exceptionally (colloq.)	1
本来	běnlái	adv.	originally；at first	3
本人	běnrén	n.	himself；herself	17
笨	bèn	adj.	stupid；foolish	12
甭	béng	adv.	need not；no need to	4
蹦	bèng	v.	jump	7
比……强	bǐ……qiáng		better than...	15
比不了	bǐ bu liǎo	vc.	not comparable to；not as good as	7
比得上	bǐ de shàng	vc.	compare；compete	18
比较	bǐjiào	adv.	rather	11
比如说	bǐrú shuō		for example	7
笔试	bǐshì	n.	written examination	7
毕业	bì yè	vo.	graduate	17
毕业生	bìyèshēng	n.	graduate (of a school)	15
编辑部	biānjíbù	n.	editorial department	16
遍	biàn	adj.	all over；all around (to be used after a verb as a complement)	17
遍	biàn	m.	(MW for action)	6
便宜坊	Biànyífāng	N.	(name of a restaurant)	1
标志	biāozhì	n.	sign；mark	19
表达	biǎodá	v.	express	5
表情	biǎoqíng	n.	(facial) expression	18
表示	biǎoshì	v.	express	15
表现	biǎoxiàn	v./n.	behavior；conduct	7
憋死	biē si	vc.	be suffocated to death	5
别价	biéjie	adv.	(see note 16)	2
病号	bìnghào	n.	hospitalized patient	11
病情	bìngqíng	n.	state of an illness；patient's condition	12
伯父	bófù	n.	uncle (a polite form of address for a man of one's father's generation)	15
博拉姆斯	Bólāmǔsī	N.	Johannes Brahms (19th-century German	9

			composer)	
博士	bóshì	n.	Ph. D. ; doctor's degree	14
补	bǔ	v.	nourish body; make up for	2
补品	bǔpǐn	n.	tonic	14
部	bù	n.	department (of a company)	15
不(一)定	bù (yi) dìng		no one knows; possibly	11
不成	bùchéng	part.	(It is used to attach to the end of a sentence to indicate inference or a rhetorical question)	2
不及格	bù jígé		fail (an exam); flunk	5
不仅	bùjǐn	adv.	not only	5
不客气	bú kèqì		you are welcome	1
不耐烦	bú nàifán		impatient	15
不然	bùrán	conj.	otherwise	13
不如	bùrú	v.	not as good as	9
不像话	bú xiàng huà		absurd; outrageous	11
不信(这个)邪	bú xìn (zhè ge) xié		(see note 12)	20
不要紧	bù yàojǐn		It doesn't matter	3
不止	bùzhǐ	v.	more than; not limited to	20
不至于	bú zhìyú		cannot go so far; be unlikely	20
布满	bùmǎn	vc.	be covered by	9
布置	bùzhì	v.	assign (homework, etc.)	5
部门	bùmén	n.	department; branch; section; division	7

C

裁员	cái yuán	vo.	cut staff; lay off employees	14
才智	cáizhì	n.	talent; gift	7
踩	cǎi	v.	step upon; stamp	10
采访	cǎifǎng	v.	interview	2
彩虹	cǎihóng	n.	rainbow	5
残书	cán shū		damaged book	16
惨	cǎn	adj.	miserable; tragic	18
测试	cèshì	v.	test; assessment	7
噌噌见长	cēngcēng jiànzhǎng		(see note 7)	6
差点儿	chà diǎnr		almost	2
拆封	chāi fēng	vo.	tear open the seal	13
搀	chān	v.	assist by the arm	18

初三	chū sān		Middle school 3rd year	12
处	chù	n.	place; location	5
处理不了	chǔlǐ bù liǎo	vc.	unable to handle (an issue or a matter)	11
不了	bù liǎo		(complement following a verb indicating not being able to)	
处长	chùzhǎng	n.	head of a department or office; section chief	3
穿衣戴帽	chuān yī dài mào		get dressed (literally: to put on the clothes and the hat)	11
窗户	chuānghu	n.	window	10
吹(个)风	chuī (ge) fēng	vo.	blow (hair)	10
春节	Chūn Jié	N.	Spring Festival; Chinese New Year	19
纯情	chúnqíng	n.	pure feeling; innocent love	5
此地	cǐ dì		this place; here	9
聪明	cōngmíng	adj./n.	intelligent, wise; intelligence, wisdom	7
村	cūn	n.	village	18
撮一顿	cuō yi dùn	vo.	have a good meal	6
错怪	cuòguài	v.	wrong (someone)	4
错误	cuòwù	n.	mistake; error	4

D

搭理	dāli	v.	(usu. used in the negative) respond; answer	20
答应	dāying	v.	answer; respond	12
打(个)折	dǎ (ge) zhé	vo.	allow a discount	16
打扮	dǎban	n./v.	dress, what one wears; dress up, make up	11
打饱嗝	dǎ bǎogé	vo.	belch	6
打岔	dǎ chà	vo.	interrupt (one's speech)	15
打断	dǎ duàn	vc.	interrupt (a speech, an action, etc.)	15
打工	dǎ gōng	vo.	have a temporary job; do manual work	18
打开	dǎ kāi	vc.	open	7
打联联	dǎliánlián	v.	associate with someone	18
打水漂	dǎ shuǐpiāo	vo.	(see note 9)	2
大大	dàda	n.	(child's form of address for any man elder than his/her father) uncle; father's older brother (mostly used in the Northern dialect)	10

大哥	dàgē	n.	older brother (form of address for a man about one's own age)	11
大街	dàjiē	n.	main street	17
大姐	dàjiě	n.	eldest sister (a form of address for a woman about one.'s own age)	11
大款	dàkuǎn	n.	person of wealth (colloq.)	9
大妈	dàmā	n.	aunt (an affectionate or respectful form of address for an elderly woman); father's elder brother's wife	19
大名鼎鼎	dàmíng dǐngdǐng		famous; well-known; celebrated	15
大人	dàren	n.	adult; grown up	4
大嫂	dàsǎo	n.	older brother's wife (form of address for a married woman about one's own age)	11
大声	dà shēng		loudly; in loud voice	7
大谈特谈	dà tán tè tán		speak (on a topic) extensively and heartily	15
大爷	dàye	n.	uncle (a respectful form of address for an elderly man); father's elder brother	2
待会儿	dāi huìr		stay for a moment; wait a moment	3
待会儿	dāi huìr		wait for a minute	10
待会儿见	dāi huìr jiàn		see you later	6
逮	dǎi	v.	catch; get hold of	13
代表	dàibiǎo	v.	represent; be on behalf of	3
待人接物	dài rén jiē wù		codes of conduct; codes of behavior	6
带走	dài zǒu	vc.	take away	16
单词	dāncí	n.	vocabulary	6
单单	dāndān	adv.	only; solely	9
耽误	dānwu	v.	delay; make worse because of delay	8
胆小	dǎn xiǎo		timid	3
蛋糕	dàngāo	n.	cake	1
当初	dāngchū	t.	in the beginning; at first	10
当年	dāngnián	t.	that year (in the past)	5
当中	dāngzhōng	n.	in the midst of; during	15
当成	dàng chéng	vc.	take (someone) for (someone else)	11
导师	dǎoshī	n.	mentor; adviser	5
倒	dào	adv.	(indicating that sth. is not what one	2

			thinks)	
倒是	dàoshì	adv.	but instead; used to express what is contrary to facts	10
道	dào	m.	(a measure word for lines, stripes, rainbows, etc.)	5
道	dào	n.	stripe	11
到底	dàodǐ	adv.	after all	12
道理	dào·lǐ	n.	truth; reason	9
道歉	dào qiàn	vo.	apologize; make an apology	4
得病	dé bìng	vo.	suffer from (disease); become ill	12
得了	dé le	v.	enough of it (used to stop the other person from continuing to say or do something)	13
灯火	dēnghuǒ	n.	lights	5
登门	dēng mén	vo.	pay a visit to someone's house	3
等于	děngyú	v.	equal to; equivalent to	12
地道	dìdao	adj.	genuine; authentic	1
地儿	dìr	n.	place (colloq.)	1
地球	dìqiú	n.	earth	12
典故	diǎngù	n.	allusion; literary quotation	16
电汇	diànhuì	v.	transfer money telegraphically	9
垫上	diàn shang	vc.	pay for someone and get reimbursed later	13
掉	diào	v.	drop; fall	13
调查	diàochá	v.	investigate	9
盯紧	dīng jǐn	vc.	keep an eye on (somebody) closely; watch	11
顶多	dǐng duō		at most	13
丢人现眼	diū rén xiàn yǎn		lose face; be embarrassed	16
懂得	dǒngde	v.	understand; know	15
懂事	dǒng shì	vo.	be sensible; intelligent	10
动	dòng	v.	touch	10
动作	dòngzuò	n.	movement; motion; action	20
兜	dōu	n.	pocket	2
兜(着)	dōu (zhe)	v.	(see note 11)	9
逗	dòu	adj./v.	amusing, funny; amuse	1
豆腐块	dòufukuài	n.	(see note 5)	16
独立	dúlì	adj.	independent; on one's own	14

读研	dú yán	vo.	study as a graduate student	5
读者	dúzhě	n.	reader	16
赌气	dǔ qì	vo.	feel wronged and act rashly	4
短文	duǎnwén	n.	short article; essay	16
短信	duǎnxìn	n.	short message (on a cell phone)	7
段	duàn	m.	section; paragraph; passage	5
对不住	duì bu zhù	vc.	be sorry; apologize to	11
对方	duìfāng	n.	the other person; the other side (in a conversation, negotiation, etc.)	15
对口	duìkǒu	adj.	(see note 8)	7
对门	duìmén	n.	across the hallway; (of two apartments) facing each other	6
对手	duìshǒu	n.	opponent; adversary	15
对外	duìwài		to the public	15
顿	dùn	m.	(a measure word for meals)	15
多事	duō shì	vo.	meddle	9
多谢	duō xiè		many thanks; thanks a lot	13
朵	duǒ	m.	measure word for flowers	18

E

恶心	ěxin	adj./v.	disgusting	10
饿	è	adj.	hungry	6
而是	érshì	conj.	but (rather)	12
而言	ér yán		(used in the pattern 对……而言 duì....ér yán: in regard to...; also see note 12)	15
二十万	èrshí wàn	num.	two hundred thousand	9

F

发表	fābiǎo	v.	publish (articles, etc.)	16
发财	fā cái	vo.	get rich; make a fortune	7
发誓	fā shì	vo.	swear; vow	4
发现	fāxiàn	v.	find out	4
发展	fāzhǎn	v.	develop; advance	12
翻	fān	v.	turn over; turn up	4
反应过来	fǎnyìng guolai	vc.	realize	8
反正	fǎnzhèng	adv.	anyway; in any case	6

犯	fàn	v.	make (a mistake) ; commit (a crime)	4
方便面	fāngbiànmiàn	n.	instant noodles	15
方面	fāngmiàn	n.	aspect; field	15
方式	fāngshì	n.	way; style	6
放心	fàng xīn	vo.	rest assured; not to worry	3
非要	fēi yào		must; be determined (to do something)	9
废话	fèihuà	n.	nonsense	11
费尽心思	fèi jìn xīnsi		(see note 8)	17
分布	fēnbù	v.	distribute (over an area)	17
份	fèn	m.	(a measure word for jobs)	17
风度	fēngdù	n.	posture; bearing	19
风度扣	fēngdùkòu	n.	decorative button on a jacket	19
风土人情	fēng tǔ rén qíng		local costumes	6
缝里	fèng li		chink	13
夫人	fūren	n.	Mrs; wife	6
扶	fú	v.	support with the hand	11
福尔摩斯	Fú'ěrmósī	n.	Sherlock Holmes（a detective in the works of the 19th-century English novelist Arthur Conan Doyle）	9
福气	fúqi	n.	good luck; good fortune	18
妇女	fùnǚ	n.	woman	11
复试	fùshì	n.	re-exam; second-round exam	7
复制	fùzhì	v.	copy	5

G

该	gāi	adv.	ought to; should	4
改	gǎi	v.	change; correct	4
改编	gǎibiān	v.	adapt	17
改口	gǎi kǒu	vo.	(see note 1)	20
改天	gǎitiān	adv.	another day; some other day	16
钙	gài	n.	calcium	12
概念	gàiniàn	n.	concept	4
尴尬	gāngà	adj.	awkward; embarrassing	14
敢	gǎn	modal.	dare	3
感觉	gǎnjué	n.	feeling	5
赶紧	gǎnjǐn	adv.	hurry up	2
敢情	gǎnqing		(see note 15)	13

感情	gǎnqíng	n.	feeling; affection	14
感谢	gǎnxiè	v.	thank for; be grateful for	7
干	gàn	v.	do; work	5
干活儿	gàn huór	vo.	work; labor	18
干嘛	gànmá	pron.	for what; what to do (colloq.)	5
干吗	gànmá	pron.	why; what for	3
干什么	gàn shénme		why; what to do	3
刚好	gānghǎo	adj.	just right (as used in this story)	4
钢蹦儿	gāngbèngr	n.	coin (colloq.)	9
钢琴	gāngqín	n.	piano	17
高考	gāokǎo	n.	college or university entrance examination	12
高三	gāo sān		High school senior	12
高声	gāo shēng		loud; loudly	7
高手	gāoshǒu	n.	master hand	5
高校	gāoxiào	n.	college; university	3
搞	gǎo	v.	make	3
搞错	gǎo cuò	vc.	make a mistake	20
稿费	gǎofèi	n.	author's remuneration	16
告别	gàobié	v.	bid farewell to; say goodbye to	12
告示	gàoshi	n.	official notice	16
搁	gē	v.	put; place	2
哥儿俩	gēr liǎ		two buddies	13
哥们儿	gēmenr	n.	buddy; pal (colloq.)	7
搁着过去	gēzhe guòqù		in the past (colloq.)	20
格调	gédiào	n.	style	9
各位	gè wèi		everybody; you-all	20
根本	gēnběn	adv.	absolutely; fundamentally	9
根据	gēnjù	prep.	based on	17
公安局	gōng'ānjú	n.	police station; public security bureau	9
宫殿	gōngdiàn	n.	palace	1
工会	gōnghuì	n.	labor union; trade union	3
公交车	gōngjiāochē	n.	vehicle of public transportation	7
恭喜	gōngxǐ	v.	congratulate	7
共进晚餐	gòng jìn wǎncān		eat dinner together	6
共享	gòngxiǎng	v.	share; sharing	5
购买	gòumǎi	v.	buy; purchase	16

姑奶奶	gūnǎinai	n.	grandaunt	9
姑娘	gūniang	n.	girl; daughter	10
古人	gǔrén	n.	ancients; forefathers	12
顾	gù	v.	care for	18
顾	gù	v.	pay attention to	20
顾客	gùkè	n.	customer; shopper	16
顾全大局	gùquán dàjú		(see note 9)	7
故宫	Gùgōng	N.	Imperial Palace	1
故事	gùshi	n.	story	1
故意	gùyì	adv.	intentionally; deliberately	8
挂	guà	v.	hang	5
挂炉	guàlú	n.	(a kind of stove for roasting duck)	1
乖	guāi	adj.	(of a child) obedient; well behaved; be good	4
怪	guài	adv.	very; quite	3
怪不得	guàibude		no wonder; so that's why	13
观点	guāndiǎn	n.	point of view; standpoint	11
关系	guān·xì	n.	relation; relationship; relevance	7
关心	guānxīn	v.	care; concern (for someone)	17
关于	guānyú	prep.	about; pertaining to; concerning	15
官园	Guānyuán	n.	(name of a market)	20
管	guǎn	prep.	from (sb.)	2
光	guāng	adv.	only; merely	5
逛街	guàng jiē	vo.	go sightseeing on streets; go window-shopping	19
闺女	guīnü	n.	daughter	3
鬼点子	guǐdiǎnzi	n.	tricky ideas	19
国安	Guó'ān	n.	(name of a football team)	20
国货	guóhuò	n.	product of one's own country	19
过不了	guò bu liǎo	vc.	unable to pass	3
过程	guòchéng	n.	course of events; process	15
过分	guòfèn	adj.	excessive	11
过门	guò mén	vo.	(of a woman) get married into the husband's family	18
过意不去	guòyì bu qù		(see note 7)	12

H

咳	hāi	interj.	(an exclamation)	2
海边	hǎibiān	n.	seashore	11
害	hài	v.	impair; cause trouble to	7
憨憨	Hānhān	N.	(name of a dog)	10
含蓄	hánxù	adj.	subtle; reserved	6
寒碜	hánchen	adj.	ugly	10
寒暄	hánxuān	v.	exchange of pleasantries	15
涵养	hányǎng	n.	self restraint; virtue of patience; accomplishment in self cultivation	15
汉语	Hànyǔ	N.	Chinese language	1
行业	hángyè	n.	trade; profession	17
好几天	hǎo jǐ tiān		quite a few days	2
好家伙	hǎo jiāhuo		(see note 2)	18
好了	hǎo le		OK; that's enough	3
好嘞	hǎo lei		alright	13
好日子	hǎo rìzi		auspicious date; happy occasion	3
好使	hǎoshǐ	adj.	effective	19
好受	hǎoshòu	adj.	comfortable	5
好像	hǎoxiàng	v.	seem like	9
好意思	hǎo yìsi		have the nerve (to do something improper)	15
好友	hǎo yǒu		good friend	20
耗子	hàozi	n.	mouse; rat	7
盒	hé	n.	box	14
荷兰	Hélán	N.	the Netherlands; Holland	7
河南	Hénán	N.	Henan (a province in China)	7
合同	hétong	n.	agreement; contract	9
嗨	hēi	interj.	(used to call attention) hey	8
嘿	hei	interj.	(used to call attention)	5
嘿嘿	hēihēi	ono.	(onomatopoeia for the sound of laughter)	13
哼	hēng	interj.	Hmph	2
红烧	hóngshāo	v.	braise (meat)	2
后果	hòuguǒ	n.	consequence	9
后悔	hòuhuǐ	v.	regret	12
后面	hòumian	n.	at the back; behind	2
壶	hú	n.	kettle; pot	2

胡嘞嘞	húlēle	v.	speak nonsense；nonsense	18
花园	huāyuán	n.	garden	3
划拉	huála	v.	scribble	5
化疗	huàliáo	n. /v	chemotherapy	12
画外音	huà wài yīn	n.	off screen voice (in film or TV)	7
怀疑	huáiyí	v.	suspect；doubt	4
荒郊野外	huāngjiāo yěwài		wilderness	9
晃	huǎng	v.	sway	20
晃动	huǎngdòng	v.	rock；sway	20
（上）回	(shàng) huí	m.	last time (same as 上次)	2
回首	huí shǒu	vo.	turn one's head；turn around (literary)	5
回头	huí tóu	vo.	turn round；look back；trun back	13
毁	huǐ	v.	damage；ruin	18
汇款	huìkuǎn	n. /v.	remittance	9
会面	huì miàn	vo.	meet	19
汇票	huìpiào	n.	money order	9
浑身	húnshēn	n.	from head to toe；all over	11
混	hùn	v.	(see note 3)	7
活人	huórén	n.	living person	5
货	huò	n.	goods；commodity	13

J

基础	jīchǔ	n.	foundation, basis	15
几乎	jīhū	adv.	almost；nearly	17
机会	jīhuì	n.	opportunity	7
激烈	jīliè	adj.	intense；acute；fierce	17
及时	jíshí	adj.	timely, in time；promptly	17
记	jì	v.	remember	15
记起来	jì qilai	vc.	remember；recall	16
记性	jìxing	n.	memory	4
计较	jìjiào	v.	discuss in minute detail；argue；dispute	8
既然	jìrán	conj.	since；now that	9
技术	jìshù	n.	technology；skill	7
技术员	jìshùyuán	n.	technician	14
寂寞	jìmò	adj.	lonely；lonesome	10
家	jiā	m.	(measure word for business establishments)	1

家常便饭	jiācháng biànfàn		homely food	6
家常菜	jiācháng cài	n.	homely dish	6
家具	jiājù	n.	furniture	9
家长	jiāzhǎng	n.	parent or guardian of a child	4
加倍	jiābèi	adv.	doubly	17
加起来	jiā qilai	vc.	total; add together	8
夹	jiā	v.	put in between	14
假	jiǎ	adj.	fake; false	8
假币	jiǎbì	n.	fake money; counterfeit	8
假不了	jiǎ bu liǎo	vc.	cannot be fake	8
假钱	jiǎ qián	n.	fake money	8
假装	jiǎzhuāng	v.	pretend	8
肩膀	jiānbǎng	n.	shoulder	18
捡	jiǎn	v.	pick up	10
剪	jiǎn	v.	cut（with scissors）	19
捡回来	jiǎn huílai	vc.	pick up	12
健全	jiànquán	adj.	healthy; sound	17
健全人	jiànquán rén		healthy person	17
将	jiāng	prep.	（a more formal equivalent of the preposition 把）	9
讲	jiǎng	v.	pay attention to	2
讲（点儿）规矩	jiǎng (diǎnr) guīju	vo.	go by the rules	11
讲究	jiǎngjiu	v./n.	pay attention to; be particular about; be fussy about	1
交	jiāo	v.	hand in	5
交流	jiāoliú	v.	communicate	17
交谈	jiāotán	v.	talk; converse	15
叫法	jiàofǎ	n.	the way one addresses someone	10
教诲	jiàohuì	v.	teaching; instruction; advice	7
教师	jiàoshī	n.	teacher	1
教训	jiàoxun	v.	lesson	8
教育	jiàoyù	v.	teach; educate	4
街	jiē	n.	street	18
接触	jiēchù	v.	contact	15
街坊	jiēfang	n.	neighbor	10
接受	jiēshòu	v.	accept	6

结果	jiéguǒ	n./conj.	result; outcome	14
结（了）婚	jié (le) hūn	vo.	get married	3
结了	jié le		(see note 11)	2
解馋	jiě chán	vo.	(see note 3)	2
斤	jīn	m.	of weight (equal to 1/2 kilogram)	8
今儿	jīnr	t.	today (colloq.)	1
紧紧	jǐnjǐn		closely; tightly	15
谨慎	jǐnshèn	adj.	prudent; careful; cautious; circumspect	17
尽	jìn	adv.	completely	20
进行	jìnxíng	v.	carry on; carry out; conduct	7
尽快	jǐnkuài	adv.	as quickly (soon) as possible	8
进入	jìnrù	v.	enter; get into	5
经常	jīngcháng	adv.	often; regularly	1
经过	jīngguò	v./n.	based on; as a result of	14
京郊	Jīngjiāo	N.	suburbs or outskirts of Beijing	18
经理	jīnglǐ	n.	manager	7
经历	jīnglì	n.	experience	17
精神	jīngshen	adj.	lively; vigorous	10
惊喜	jīngxǐ	n.	pleasant surprise	3
警察	jǐngchá	n.	police	9
净	jìng	adv.	purely; completely	3
竞	jìng	v.	compete; contest	14
竞标	jìng biāo	vo.	competitive bidding	14
竞争	jìngzhēng	v.	compete	7
救命恩人	jiùmìng ēnrén		savior	18
居然	jūrán	adv.	unexpectedly; to one's surprise	12
句	jù	m.	(a measure word for speech)	6
剧	jù	n.	play	17
距离	jùlí	n.	distance; disparity	7
据我所知	jù wǒ suǒ zhī		to my knowledge	5
句子	jùzi	n.	sentence	6
娟子	Juānzi	N.	(a nickname for Chen Juan)	15
决定	juédìng	v.	decide	14
绝对	juéduì	adv.	Absolutely	4
绝了	jué le		beyond compare	5
觉着	juézhe	v.	feel	3

K

卡	kǎ	n.	card；credit card	9
开口	kāi kǒu	vo.	open one's mouth；start to talk	4
开玩笑	kāi wánxiào	vo.	joke；make fun	17
开张	kāizhāng	v.	open for business	13
看出来	kàn chulai	vc.	make out；see	12
看法	kàn·fǎ	n.	opinion；point of view	5
看来	kàn lái		it appears；it seems	5
看上去	kàn shangqu		look like	11
看重	kànzhòng	v.	value；think highly of	7
烤	kǎo	v.	bake；roast；toast；broil	1
考察	kǎochá	v.	inspect；observe and study	14
考官	kǎoguān	n.	interviewer	15
考虑	kǎolǜ	v.	consider；think about	3
考验	kǎoyàn	v./n.	ordeal；test	7
烤鸭	kǎoyā	n.	roast duck	1
烤鸭店	kǎoyā diàn	n.	roast duck restaurant	1
靠	kào	v.	depend on；rely on	14
可不是	kěbushì	adv.	(I) can't agree with you more；I totally agree with you	18
客户	kèhù	n.	client；customer	15
肯定	kěndìng	adv.	certainly；definitely	2
坑	kēng	v.	ruin (as used in this story)；entrap	18
吭	kēng	v.	utter a sound or a word	10
口味	kǒuwèi	n.	(of food) taste；flavor	1
扣	kòu	v.	button up	19
扣子	kòuzi	n.	button	19
夸奖	kuājiǎng	v.	praise；compliment；commend	17
夸张	kuāzhāng	adj.	exaggerated	10
快	kuài	adj.	(of a knife, spear, etc.) sharp	15
快快乐乐	kuài kuài lè lè		happily	12
款	kuǎn	n.	money；cash	16

L

| 拉 | lā | v. | (of a driver) drive (somebody) | 1 |
| 邋遢 | lāta | adj. | slovenly；sloppy | 11 |

来到	lái dào	vc.	come to; arrive at	17
阑珊	lánshān	v.	waning; coming to an end (literary)	5
浪漫	làngmàn	adj.	romantic; unconventional	3
老爸	lǎobà	n.	(a colloquial form of address for father)	19
老板	lǎobǎn	n.	boss; manager; shopkeeper	8
老伴儿	lǎobànr	n.	husband or wife (of an old married couple)	2
老北京	lǎo běijīng		person who has lived in Beijing for a long time and knows the city thoroughly	1
老弟	lǎodì	n.	young fellow（a form of address for a male adult younger than oneself)	13
老公	lǎogōng	n.	husband（colloquial term）	10
老妈	lǎomā	n.	(a colloquial form of address for mother)	19
老奶奶	lǎonǎinai	n.	grandmother; granny	10
老年	lǎonián	n.	(of a person) old; old age	7
老朋友	lǎo péngyou		old friend	1
老婆	lǎopó	n.	wife	6
老人家	lǎorénjiā	n.	(an respectful form of address for an old person)	3
老头子	lǎotóuzi	n.	old man，husband（wife's term of address for her old husband）	8
老外	lǎowài	n.	foreigner	20
老兄	lǎoxiōng	n.	buddy; pal（colloq.）	7
老爷子	lǎoyézi	n.	old man; elderly person	8
老子	lǎozi	n.	father (colloquial expression)	4
姥姥	lǎolao	n.	(maternal) grandmother	4
姥姥	lǎolao		(see note 14)	20
乐趣	lèqù	n.	joy; pleasure	12
了解	liǎojiě	v.	understand; know (sb) well	4
愣	lèng	adv.	insist on	9
黎明公司	Límíng Gōngsī	n.	Daybreak Company (a company's name)	15
礼拜	lǐbài	n.	week	20
里边	lǐbian	n.	inside; within	17
理工大学附中	Lǐgōng Dàxué Fùzhōng	n.	High school affiliated to University of Science and Technology	12
礼貌	lǐmào	n.	courtesy; politeness	16
礼品	lǐpǐn	n.	gift; present	14

礼仪	lǐyí	n.	etiquette	15
理由	lǐyóu	n.	reason; justification	17
厉害	lìhai	adj.	formidable; powerful	5
立马	lìmǎ	adv.	immediately	11
利用	lìyòng	v.	make use of; take advantage of	6
联系	liánxì	v.	contact; get in touch with	16
连续	liánxù	v.	successive; continuous	20
良师出 高徒	liáng shī chū gāo tú		a great teachers produces brilliant students; the teacher of enlightenment brings up disciples of accomplishment	6
良心	liángxīn	n.	conscience	9
两口子	liǎngkǒuzi	n.	husband and wife; married couple	6
两下子	liǎng xiàzi		(see note 1)	9
料子	liàozi	n.	fabric	19
邻居	línjū	n.	neighbor; people of the neighborhood	6
临阵磨枪	lín zhèn mó qiāng		(see note 2)	15
翎子	Língzi	n.	a person's given name	19
领带	lǐngdài	n.	necktie; tie	19
领导	lǐngdǎo	n.	leader; superior	11
领(个)证	lǐng (ge) zhèng	vo.	apply the certificate; receive the certificate	3
令人失望	lìng rén shīwàng		disappointing	7
溜溜	liūliū	adv.	(see note 4)	20
留点儿神	liú diǎnr shén		be careful; be mindful	18
喽	lou	interj.	a sentence particle, same as 了 here	10
搂	lǒu	v.	hold in one's arms; hug; embrace	18
漏	lòu	v.	leak; let out	13
露两手	lòu liǎng shǒu		(see note 5)	6
露怯	lòu qiè	vo.	(see note 5)	19
炉火	lúhuǒ	n.	stove fire	1
录用	lùyòng	v.	employ; hire	7
乱	luàn	adj.	indiscriminately (as used in this context)	10
乱七八糟	luàn qi bā zāo	adj.	in a mess; mess up	16
轮不到	lún bu dào	vc.	it (usu. a good thing) won't come one's way	14
论文	lùnwén	n.	thesis; dissertation; paper	5
摞	luò	m.	pile; stack	15

| 旅游 | lǚyóu | v. | travel；tour | 1 |

M

嘛	ma	part.	(used to emphasize the obvious)	2
麻利	máli	adj.	quick	3
马虎	mǎhu	adj.	careless；negligent	13
马夹	mǎjiá	n.	vest	11
马路	mǎlù	n.	street	11
骂人	mà rén	vo.	swear (at people)	20
买不着	mǎi bu zháo	vc.	unable to buy (something)	11
买卖人	mǎimairén	n.	businessman	13
满分	mǎn fēn		full score	5
满意	mǎnyì	adj.	satisfied；pleased	17
慢用	màn yòng		eat casually；take your time	1
慢走	màn zǒu		take care	16
盲人	mángrén	n.	blind person；the blind	17
毛病	máobìng	n.	disease；illness；shortcoming (a fault in sb's character)	18
冒傻气	mào shǎqì	vo.	(see note 6)	2
么	me	p.	(question-end particle equivalent to 吗)	13
没法	méi fǎ		unable	5
没法说	méi fǎ shuō		can't describe	20
没准儿	méi zhǔnr	v.	不一定；perhaps；probably	15
美丽	měilì	adj.	beautiful	17
美食	měishí	n.	delicious food；delicacies	1
美姿美仪	měi zī měi yí		(see note 1)	19
昧	mèi	v.	conceal	9
昧良心	mèi liángxīn	vo.	go against one's conscience	8
闷炉	mènlú	n.	(a kind of stove for roasting duck)	1
蒙在鼓里	méng zài gǔ li		be kept in the dark	18
孟	Mèng	N.	(a surname)	18
梦想成真	mèng xiǎng chéng zhēn		a dream come true	17
密	mì	adj.	dense；thick (also see note 9)	15
秘诀	mìjué	n.	secret of success；knack	5
秘书	mìshū	n.	secretary	7
免得	miǎnde	conj.	so as not to；so as to avoid	20
面包虫	miànbāochóng	n.	(a kind of insect)	20

面对	miànduì	v.	face; confront	15
面前	miàn qián		in front of	12
面试	miànshì	v./n.	interview	15
面条儿	miàntiáor	n.	noodles	1
描述	miáoshù	v.	describe	11
名吃	míngchī	n.	famous food	1
名额	míng'é	n.	quota of people	14
名牌	míngpái	n.	brand name	19
名片	míngpiàn	n.	business card	9
名誉	míngyù	n.	reputation; fame	18
明白	míngbai	v./adj.	understand; come to see; clear	7
明亮	míngliàng	adj.	well lit; bright	12
明明	míngmíng	adv.	obviously; simply	4
命脉	mìngmài	n.	lifeline	15
命运	mìngyùn	n.	destiny; fate	12
蓦然	mòrán	adv.	suddenly; abruptly	5
陌生	mòshēng	adj.	unknown; unfamiliar	7
陌生人	mòshēng rén	n.	stranger	3
默认	mòrèn	v.	give tacit consent to; tacitly approve	12
某	mǒu	pron.	certain; indefinite (person or thing)	7
母亲	mǔqin	n.	mother	3
目击	mùjī	v.	witness	9

N

嗯	ǹ	interj.	(an exclamation)	3
拿下	ná xià	vc.	capture; seize (also see note 3)	13
拿走	ná zǒu	vc.	take away	9
哪儿有的事	nǎr yǒu de shì		that's nonsense	3
那样	nàyàng	pron.	that way; like that	16
难道	nándào	adv.	Is it possible that...; Do you really mean to say that...	6
难度	nándù	n.	degree of difficulty	13
难能可贵	nán néng kě guì		(see note 9)	17
南京	Nánjīng	N.	Nanjing (capital of Jiangsu Province)	15
男子汉	nánzǐhàn	n.	a real man; true man	12
脑	nǎo	n.	brain; head	3
脑袋	nǎodai	n.	head	18

闹	nào	v.	make a fuss	11
闹出事	nào chū shì		be in trouble；have an accident	18
闹肚子	nào dùzi	vo.	have diarrhea	10
闹了半天	nào le bàn tiān		(see note 10)	10
闹（大）笑话	nào（dà）xiàohua	vo.	become the laughing stock；make a fool of oneself	19
能否	néng fǒu		possible or not；able or not；whether	7
能力	nénglì	n.	ability；talent	7
尼诺里拉	Nínuòlǐlā	N.	Ninoriva (an Italian brand)	19
年纪轻	niánjì qīng		young	8
年轻	niánqīng	adj.	young	3
年轻有为	niánqīng yǒuwéi		young and promising	14
鸟	niǎo	n.	bird	20
鸟食	niǎo shí	n.	food for birds	20
尿	niào	n.	urine	5
宁静	níngjìng	adj.	peaceful and tranquil	7
扭头	niǔ tóu	vo.	turn around	13
农民	nóngmín	n.	peasant	18
弄	nòng	v.	do；handle；deal with (colloq.)	5
弄丢	nòng diū	vc.	lose；mislay	5
努力	nǔlì	adj./v.	make efforts；try hard	14
女士	nǚshì	n.	lady；madam	6

O

噢	ō	interj.	(suggesting surprised understanding)	1
欧式	ōushì	adj.	of European style	9
O 型血	Ou xíng xuè		O Type blood	12
偶然	ǒurán	adv./adj.	accidentally	16

P

排	pái	v.	rank	5
牌儿	páir	n.	brand (colloq.)	19
派	pài	v.	send；dispatch	14
陪	péi	v.	accompany	13
赔不是	péi búshì	vo.	apologize	18
赔礼道歉	péi lǐ dào qiàn		apologize	18
培训	péixùn	v.	train；training	19

培养	péiyǎng	v.	foster; cultivate	17
配	pèi	v.	match (color, style, etc.)	10
烹调	pēngtiáo	v.	cook	6
碰见	pèng jiàn	vc.	meet unexpectedly; run into	5
碰巧	pèngqiǎo	adj.	coincident	10
批评	pīpíng	v.	criticize	15
脾气	píqi	n.	temperament; disposition	15
辟谣	pì yáo	vo.	refute a rumor	18
偏僻	piānpì	adj.	remote; out of the way	9
骗子	piànzi	n.	swindler; cheater	2
品位	pǐnwèi	n.	rank; grade; status	9
聘用	pìnyòng	v.	hire; employ	15
凭	píng	prep.	with (the authority or quality of)	7
平房	píngfáng	n.	bungalow	15
平时	píngshí	t.	ordinarily; normally	10
评价	píngjià	v./n.	appraise, ssess; appraisal, assessment	5

Q

欺骗	qīpiàn	v.	cheat; deceive	5
妻子	qīzi	n.	wife	6
奇了怪了	qí le guài le		(see note 3)	6
其实	qíshí	adv.	as a matter of fact; actually	4
其中	qízhōng	n.	amid it; among them	5
起(什么)哄	qǐ (shénme) hòng	vo.	kick up a fuss; stir up a disturbance	7
起码	qǐmǎ	adj.	the least; at least	15
启事	qǐshì	n.	notice; announcement	16
企业	qǐyè	n.	enterprise; business; company	15
岂有此理	qǐ yǒu cǐ lǐ		ridiculous; nonsense	10
千万	qiānwàn	adv.	by all means; absolutely; (of an admonition) must	14
钱	qián	n.	money	2
钱包	qiánbāo	n.	purse; wallet	2
浅蓝色	qiǎnlánsè	n.	light blue	11
枪口	qiāngkǒu	n.	gun (also see note 9)	14
抢	qiǎng	v.	fight (with someone over something, as used in this story)	10
悄悄	qiāo qiāo	adv.	quietly	12

瞧	qiáo	v.	look	2
瞧好儿吧	qiáo hǎor bā		(see note 2)	8
瞧瞧	qiáo qiao		look; see	18
憔悴	qiáocuì	adj.	haggard, sallow; pined away	5
亲眼	qīnyǎn	adv.	(see) with one's own eyes; (witness) personally	18
琴行	qínháng	n.	piano store	17
青年	qīngnián	n.	youth; young person	9
轻巧	qīng·qiǎo	adj.	simple; easy	2
青青	Qīngqīng	N.	(a nickname for Lü Qing)	9
青山医院	Qīngshān Yīyuàn	n.	Green Hill Hospital	11
轻松	qīngsōng	adj.	relaxed	12
轻易	qīngyì	adv.	easily; lightly	5
倾听	qīngtīng	v.	heed; listen attentively to	15
清香	qīngxiāng	adj.	delicately fragrant	1
情书	qíngshū	n.	love letter	5
情调	qíngdiào	n.	sentiment; taste	3
请教	qǐngjiào	v.	consult; seek advice from	19
请示	qǐngshì	v.	ask for or request instructions	16
请勿	qǐng wù		please do not (literary)	7
求	qiú	v.	beg	10
求职	qiú zhí	vo.	seek employment; apply for a job	17
取	qǔ	v.	take; get; fetch	16
取证	qǔ zhèng	vo.	collect evidence	9
曲子	qǔzi	n.	tune; song; melody	17
全	quán	adv.	completely; entirely	7
全部	quánbù		totality; entirety	3
全聚德	Quánjùdé	N.	(name of a restaurant)	1
全选	quán xuǎn		select all	5
缺	quē	v.	be short of; lack	4
缺德	quē dé	vo.	have no regard for other members of society; wicked	16
缺页	quē yè	vo.	missing page	16
确实	quèshí	adv.	indeed; truly	9

R

| 饶 | ráo | v. | forgive; spare | 11 |

热情	rèqíng	adj.	passionate; warm-hearted	1
人才	réncái	n.	person of ability and talent	7
人家	rénjia	pron.	sb. else; other people	2
人品	rénpǐn	n.	moral character	7
人生	rénshēng	n.	life; human life	17
人员	rényuán	n.	personnel; staff	14
认错	rèn cuò	vo.	admit a mistake; apologize	4
认清	rèn qīng	vc.	recognize; see clearly	11
认为	rènwéi	v.	consider; regard	15
认真	rènzhēn	adj.	serious	2
任何	rènhé	pron.	any	7
扔	rēng	v.	throw; throw away	9
日子	rìzi	n.	day; days	2
肉铺	ròupù	n.	meat shop	8
如此	rúcǐ	pron.	such; this kind of	5
如今	rújīn	t.	nowadays; now; today; at present	15
如愿以偿	rú yuàn yǐ cháng		have one's wishes fulfilled	17

S

嗓门儿	sǎngménr	n.	voice	7
嫂(子)	sǎo (zi)	n.	elder brother's wife (a respectful form of address for a woman who is usually older than the speaker); elder sister-in-law	18
色彩	sècǎi	n.	color	17
杀	shā	v.	kill	11
啥	shá	pron.	what; whatever	7
傻	shǎ	adj.	stupid; foolish	14
晒太阳	shài tàiyáng	vo.	sun bathe	12
商标	shāngbiāo	n.	trademark; brand mark	19
商海	shānghǎi	n.	business world	15
商量	shāngliang	v.	discuss; talk over with sb.	2
上百	shàng bǎi		reach one hundred	16
上班	shàng bān	vo.	go to work	17
上车	shàng chē	vo.	get in the car (or on the bus or train)	1
上当	shàng dàng	vo.	be fooled	8
上岗	shàng gǎng	vo.	take over a shift; begin to work	13
上缴	shàngjiǎo	v.	turn over (to a higher authority)	8

上门	shàngmén	v.	drop in; visit	16
捎	shāo	v.	send (a message)	3
少见	shǎo jiàn	v.	haven't seen you for a while; long time no see	20
哨	shào	v.	chirp; utter sound (by a bird)	20
舌头	shétou	n.	tongue	18
舍不得	shěbude	v.	relunctant to (spend money)	16
舍得	shěde	v.	willing to part with; not grudge	19
舍友	shèyǒu	n.	dormmate; roommate	5
设计	shèjì	v.	design; plan	14
社交	shèjiāo	n.	socializing	15
深	shēn	adj.	deep; profound	14
身	shēn	m.	set (of clothes)	11
身上	shēn shang		on one's body	11
什么的	shénme de...		etc.	10
婶	shěn	n.	aunt (a respectful address to a woman about one's mother's age)	18
审美	shěnměi	v.	appreciate beauty; aesthetics; aesthetical	11
肾结石	shènjiéshí	n.	kidney stone	18
生气	shēng qì	vo.	angry; get angry	5
生意	shēngyi	n.	business	16
声音	shēngyīn	n.	voice; sound	7
省得	shěngde	v.	(see note 4)	19
盛	chéng	v.	fill	2
诗	shī	n.	poetry; verse	12
师弟	shīdì	n.	male junior fellow apprentice	17
师妹	shīmèi	n.	female junior fellow apprentice	17
失眠	shīmián	v.	suffer from insomnia	14
失去	shīqù	v.	lose; miss	7
失业	shī yè	vo.	lose one's job; be unemployed	17
失主	shīzhǔ	n.	owner (of the lost item)	9
时代	shídài	n.	age; era; epoch	5
实话	shíhuà	n.	truth	17
实话跟您说	shíhuà gēn nín shuō		tell you the truth	1
实践	shíjiàn	n./v.	practice	19
实在	shízài	adj./adv.	true; honest	6
食品	shípǐn	n.	food	1

时尚	shíshàng	n.	fashion; vogue	9
使	shǐ	v.	use; employ	2
史记	Shǐjì	N.	Records of the Historian (book name)	16
市场	shìchǎng	n.	market; marketplace	8
市场管理处	shìchǎng guǎnlǐchù		Market Management Department	8
世间	shìjiān	n.	in the world	17
事先	shìxiān	t.	in advance; beforehand	3
试用期	shìyòng qī	n.	prebation period	17
收据	shōujù	n.	receipt	9
首	shǒu	n.	head; first place	5
手包	shǒubāo	n.	handbag; purse	9
守寡	shǒu guǎ	vo.	live in widowhood	3
手机	shǒujī	n.	cell phone	7
手心	shǒuxīn	n.	palm; control	15
手艺	shǒuyì	n.	skill; craftsmanship	6
手指头	shǒuzhítou	n.	finger (colloq.)	13
守着	shǒu zhe		(see note 6)	6
寿星老儿	shòuxīnglǎor	n.	person whose birthday is being celebrated	1
书柜	shūguì	n.	bookcase	16
叔叔	shūshu	n.	(child's form of address for any young man of one generation its senior) uncle; father's younger brother	10
舒心	shūxīn	adj.	pleasant	7
属于	shǔyú	v.	belong to	3
数	shù	n.	figure; number	13
摔	shuāi	v.	cause to fall and break; knock	20
涮羊肉	shuàn yángròu		instant boiled mutton	1
双鱼座	shuāngyúzuò	n.	Pisces	12
水平	shuǐpíng	n.	level; proficiency; sophistication	5
顺路	shùnlù	adv.	in passing; while on the way	16
说不定	shuō budìng	v.	perhaps; maybe	19
说不过	shuō bu guò	vc.	not as eloquent as...	10
说道	shuōdao	v.	discuss	8
说理	shuō lǐ	vo.	argue; dispute	8
说明	shuōmíng	v.	denote; demonstrate	9
说清楚	shuō qīngchu	vc.	make clear; state clearly	8
硕士	shuòshì	n.	Master's degree (of Arts or Science)	14

撕	sī	v.	tear; rip	16
司机	sījī	n.	driver; chauffeur	1
死活	sǐhuó	adv.	anyway; no matter what	4
死亡	sǐwáng	v.	death	12
死性	sǐxing	adj.	stubborn	13
送过去	sòng guoqu	vc.	deliver/carry (something over)	4
送礼	sòng lǐ	vo.	give a present; present a gift (to sb.)	14
俗	sú	adj.	vulgar; in poor taste	14
俗话	súhuà	n.	common saying; proverb	17
素质	sùzhì	n.	quality; character	7
算错账	suàn cuò zhàng		add the sum wrong	8
随便	suíbiàn	adv.	random, casual; randomly, casually	5
随地大小便	suídì dàxiǎobiàn		relieve (oneself) anywhere	10
随时	suíshí	adv.	at any time; at all times	16
岁数	suìshu	n.	age	8
孙子	sūnzi	n.	grandson	20
锁	suǒ	v./n.	lock	2
所有	suǒyǒu	adj.	all	14

T

塌	tā	v.	fall down	12
踏实	tāshi	adj.	feel at ease; steadfast	2
摊	tān	n.	stall; vendor's stand by a road or on a square	2
摊儿	tānr	n.	stall; stand	13
谈话	tán huà	vo.	discuss; talk	14
谈判	tánpàn	v.	talk, negotiate; talk, negotiation	15
趟	tàng	m.	(measure word for a trip)	8
淘汰	táotài	v.	eliminate through selection; discard	9
陶醉	táozuì	v.	be intoxicated (with happiness)	18
讨论	tǎolùn	v./n.	discuss; discussion	14
套近乎	tào jìnhu	vo.	make friends; chum up	19
特区	tèqū	n.	special zone; special (administrative) region	14
特征	tèzhēng	n.	characteristic; feature	11
提	tí	v.	mention about	2
提醒	tíxǐng	v.	remind	19

题目	tímù	n.	topic	5
体现	tǐxiàn	v.	embody; reflect	9
替	tì	prep.	take the place of; substitue for	1
天空	tiānkōng	n.	sky	5
天真	tiānzhēn	adj.	naïve	9
条件	tiáojiàn	n.	situation; environment	6
调律	tiáolǜ	v.	tune (a piano)	17
调律师	tiáolǜshī	n.	piano tuner	17
调琴	tiáo qín	vo.	tune a piano	17
调音	tiáo yīn	vo.	tune the sound (of a piano)	17
条纹	tiáowén	n.	stripe	11
挑战	tiǎozhàn	v./n.	challenge	7
听不见	tīng bu jiàn	vc.	unable to hear; inaudible	7
听懂	tīng dǒng	vc.	understand	6
听见	tīng jiàn	vc.	hear	7
挺	tǐng	adv.	very; rather	2
通过	tōngguò	v.	pass; succeed in (an exam; etc.)	7
通知	tōngzhī	v./n.	notify; inform	11
同事	tóngshì	n.	colleague; co-worker; workmate	3
痛不欲生	tòng bú yù shēng		be overwhelmed with sorrow or grieve to the extent of wishing to die	12
痛快	tòng·kuài	adj.	to one's heart's content; to one's great satisfaction	18
偷	tōu	v.	steal	4
偷偷	tōutōu	adv.	stealthily; secretly	16
头发	tóufa	n.	hair (on the head)	11
头脑	tóunǎo	n.	brains; mind	16
透气	tòu qì	vo.	get fresh air	10
突然	tūrán	adj.	suddenly; unexpectedly	18
吐	tǔ	v.	spit	11
团支部	tuánzhībù	n.	Branch of Youth League	12
退	tuì	v.	return	16
退回去	tuì huiqu	vc.	return	16
退一步说	tuì yí bù shuō		(see note 6)	9
托	tuō	v.	entrust (somebody to do something)	5
妥协	tuǒxié	v.	compromise	10
唾沫	tuòmo	n.	saliva; spittle (see note 12)	18

W

哇啦哇啦	wāla wāla		(an onomatopoeia for loud voice)	7
外宾	wàibīn	n.	foreign guest; foreign visitor	19
外焦里嫩	wài jiāo lǐ nèn		burnt outside but tender inside	1
外教	wàijiào	n.	foreign teacher	6
外面	wài·miàn	n.	outside	2
外事	wàishì	n.	foreign affairs	19
外语	wàiyǔ	n.	foreign language	6
完全	wánquán	adv.	complete, whole; completely, wholly	5
完事	wán shì		come to an end	14
玩意儿	wányìr	n.	a little thing; toy	20
万物	wànwù	n.	myriads of things	17
万一	wànyī	adv.	in case	3
汪	wāng	ono.	(onomatopoeia; sound that dogs make)	4
网络	wǎngluò	n.	internet; network	5
为人	wéirén		behavior; conduct	17
唯一	wéiyī	adj.	single; only; sole	17
胃	wèi	n.	stomach	18
胃口	wèikǒu	n.	appetite	1
未必	wèibì	adv.	not necessarily	15
未来	wèilái	n.	future	7
文科	wénkē	n.	liberal arts; humanities	15
文明	wénmíng	n.	civil, urbane; civilization	15
文章	wénzhāng	n.	article; essay	16
文章	wénzhāng	n.	writing	5
文字	wénzì	n.	written words; writing	5
稳定	wěndìng	adj.	stable; steady	12
吻合	wěnhé	adj.	consistent with	7
握	wò	v.	hold; grasp	15
握手	wò shǒu	vo.	shake hands	15
乌鸦嘴	wūyā zuǐ		(see note 13)	18
无非	wúfēi	adv.	nothing but; no more than (also see note 11)	15
无话不谈	wú huà bù tán		keep no secret from each other	15
无论	wúlùn	conj.	whether... or...	5
误会	wùhuì	v.	misunderstand	14

X

西餐厅	xīcāntīng	n.	Western-style restaurant	19
西服	xīfú	n.	西装，Western suit	19
西服革履	xīfú gélǚ		dressed up (literally: Western suit and leather shoes)	11
西瓜	xīguā	n.	watermelon	3
西洋景	xīyángjǐng	n.	(see note 3)	20
西装	xīzhuāng	n.	Western suit	19
吸收	xīshōu	v.	absorption	12
媳妇儿	xífur	n.	wife (northern colloq.)	18
喜新厌旧	xǐ xīn yàn jiù		(see note 2)	10
细	xì	adj.	fine; thin	1
细说	xì shuō		say in detail	5
瞎	xiā	adv.	groundlessly; foolishly	2
瞎猜	xiā cāi		guess blindly	15
下班	xià bān	vo.	get off work	2
下工夫	xià gōngfu	vo.	make efforts; work hard	20
下文	xiàwén	n.	(see note 8)	2
下载	xiàzài	v.	download	5
吓唬	xiàhu	v.	frighten; scare	3
夏令营	xiàlìngyíng	n.	summer camp	4
吓着	xià zhao	vc.	frighten	10
鲜亮	xiānliàng	adj.	bright and glossy	19
先斩后奏	xiān zhǎn hòu zòu		(see note 7)	3
闲话	xiánhuà	n.	gossip	18
嫌弃	xiánqì	v.	dislike and avoid; disfavor	10
闲事	xiánshì	n.	other people's business	7
馅儿饼	xiànrbǐng	n.	pancake; pie	14
现场	xiànchǎng	n.	scene (of event or incident); site; spot	9
现成	xiànchéng	adj.	readily available	6
线索	xiànsuǒ	n.	clue; trace	11
香	xiāng	adj.	delicious	6
箱包	xiāngbāo	n.	cases; bags	13
相信	xiāngxìn	v.	believe	9
箱子	xiāngzi	n.	chest; box; case; trunk	13
想开	xiǎng kāi	vc.	take things easy; be resigned to misfortune	12

想起	xiǎng qǐ	vc.	think of；recall	5
想起来	xiǎng qilai	vc.	recall；remember	2
想一块儿去了	xiǎng yíkuàir qu le		(see note 16)	18
像…似的	xiàng…shìde		be like…	3
项目	xiàngmù	n.	project；program	14
象牙	xiàngyá	n.	ivory	11
象征	xiàngzhēng	v.	symbolize；signify	1
消	xiāo	v.	become thinner (literary)	5
消停	xiāoting	adj.	calm；uneventful	9
消息	xiāoxi	n.	news	14
小菜一碟	xiǎocài yì dié		a piece of cake (literally：a dishful of vegetable)	13
小儿科	xiǎo'érkē	n.	(see note 6)	15
小狗	xiǎogǒu	n.	little dog	4
小孩儿	xiǎoháir	n.	child；kid	20
小伙子	xiǎohuǒzi	n.	lad；young fellow	2
小卖部	xiǎomàibù	n.	small shop；convenience store	18
小气鬼	xiǎoqìguǐ	n.	mean person (as used in this story)；miser	10
小气劲儿	xiǎoqi jìnr		stingy；miserly	4
小声	xiǎoshēng	adv.	(speak) softly；whisper	7
小偷儿	xiǎotōur	n.	petty thief	9
小巷	xiǎoxiàng	n.	small alley	17
小心	xiǎoxīn	v./adj.	be careful；be cautious	10
小夜曲	xiǎoyèqǔ	n.	serenade	9
小子	xiǎozi	n.	boy；chap	18
笑话	xiàohua	v./n.	laugh at；joke	4
心病	xīnbìng	n.	worry；anxiety	13
心里	xīnli		in the heart；in the mind	2
心目中	xīnmù zhōng		in (someone's) mind's eye	17
心情	xīnqíng	n.	mood	12
心疼	xīnténg	v.	love dearly；feel sorry	2
心眼儿	xīnyǎnr	n.	intelligence；cleverness	2
心眼儿	xīnyǎnr	n.	intention；heart	18
新闻	xīnwén	n.	news；rumor	18
信儿	xìnr	n.	message	3
信封	xìnfēng	n.	envelope	13
信息	xìnxī	n.	information	15
信息时代	xìnxī shídài		IT age	15

信誉	xìnyù	n.	reputation	2
腥	xīng	adj.	fishy (smell)	14
兴	xīng	v.	have (something) in vogue	1
行了	xíng le		enough of it; stop it	5
刑事	xíngshì	adj.	criminal	9
行头	xíngtou	n.	clothing; costume	19
形象	xíngxiàng	n.	image	7
幸福	xìngfú	adj./n.	happy; happiness	3
性格	xìnggé	n.	personality	15
兴趣	xìngqù	n.	interest	17
兴致勃勃	xìngzhì bóbó		full of zest or enthusiasm; in high spirits (also see note 8)	15
凶	xiōng	adj.	vicious; fierce; mean	10
兄弟	xiōngdi	n.	(see note 12)	7
修车	xiū chē	vo.	repair bike; fix bike	2
修养	xiūyǎng	n.	cultivation	7
虚脱	xūtuō	v.	collapse	18
需要	xūyào	v./n.	need; want	16
许多	xǔduō	num.	many; much; a lot of	7
宣传委员	xuānchuán wěiyuán	n.	committee member in charge of communication and public relations	12
喧哗	xuānhuá	v.	make hubbub; make uproar	7
学而时习之不亦说乎	xué ér shí xí zhī bú yì yuè hū		"Is it not pleasant to learn with a constant perseverance and application?"	12
学费	xuéfèi	n.	tuition fee	19
学会	xué huì	vc.	learn; master	6
学士	xuéshì	n.	bachelor's degree	14
学问	xuéwen	n.	learning; knowledge; scholarship	5
血癌	xuè'ái	n.	leukemia	12

Y

压成	yā chéng	vc.	(see note 5)	16
押口	yā kǒu	vo.	(see note 16)	20
鸭子	yāzi	n.	duck; duckling	1
淹死	yān sǐ	vc.	be drowned	18
研究	yánjiū	v.	consider; deliberate	14
眼中	yǎn zhōng		in (someone's) eyes	17

演奏	yǎnzòu	v.	play (a musical instrument)	17
阳光	yángguāng	n.	sunshine	17
阳光明媚	yángguāng míngmèi		beautiful sunshine	12
腰	yāo	n.	waist; small of the back	18
邀请	yāoqǐng	v.	invite	6
摇上	yáo shàng	vc.	roll (a window) up (to close the window of a car)	10
要	yào	modal.	must	5
要不	yàobù	conj.	otherwise; or else	6
要不是	yàobushì	conj.	if it were not for	18
要面子	yào miànzi	vo.	be concerned about face saving; be sensitive about one's reputation	4
要求	yāoqiú	v.	requirement	7
钥匙	yàoshi	n.	key	2
爷爷	yéye	n.	(paternal) grandfather; grandpa	10
也许	yěxǔ	adv.	perhaps; probably; maybe	9
页	yè	m.	page	16
业务	yèwù	n.	vocational work; professional work	7
伊	yī	pron.	she; her (archaic)	5
一辈子	yí bèizi		all one's life; a lifetime	13
一旦	yídàn	adv.	in case (something happens); once	14
一气	yí qì		(see note 13)	10
一切	yíqiè	pron.	all; everything	7
一万	yíwàn	num.	ten thousand	9
一百万	yìbǎiwàn	num.	a million	9
一般	yìbān	adj.	usually	13
一身	yì shēn		whole body; (combination of) everything one wears	19
一言为定	yì yán wéi dìng		it's a deal; that's settled	19
一直	yìzhí	adv.	always; all along	3
一屋子	yì wūzi		a roomful of	19
衣裳	yīshang	n.	clothes	11
依我看	yī wǒ kàn		as I see it; in my opinion	15
依我看	yī wǒ kàn		in my opinion	20
医学	yīxué	n.	medical science; medicine	12
遗憾	yíhàn	adj.	regret; regrettable	5

以后	yǐhòu	t.	from now on; later on	6
意见	yì‧jiàn	n.	view; opinion	3
意犹未尽	yì yóu wèi jìn		not having one's meaning/emotion fully expressed	5
因小失大	yīn xiǎo shī dà		(see note 11)	7
引用	yǐnyòng	v.	quote; cite	16
鹰	yīng	n.	eagle; falcon	18
迎接	yíngjiē	v.	welcome; meet	12
影响	yǐngxiǎng		impair; interfere with; affect	7
应急	yìng jí	vo.	meet an emergency; meet an urgent need	14
应聘	yìngpìn	v.	apply (for a job)	7
营业员	yíngyèyuán	n.	store clerk; shop assistant	16
英语课代表	yīngyǔ kèdàibiǎo		monitor for English class	12
哟	yō	interj.	(expressing slight surprise)	1
勇敢	yǒnggǎn	adj.	brave; courageous	12
永远	yǒngyuǎn	adv.	always; forever	12
用不着	yòng bu zháo	vc.	not necessary; useless	12
用户	yònghù	n.	consumer	17
用语	yòngyǔ	n.	phraseology; term	15
优秀	yōuxiù	adj.	outstanding; excellent	17
由	yóu	prep.	up to (somebody to do something)	7
由于	yóuyú	prep.	as a result of; due to	16
游	yóu	v.	tour; sightsee	1
游客	yóukè	n.	traveller; tourist; sightseer	1
游泳衣	yóuyǒngyī	n.	swimming suit	11
油亮	yóuliàng	adj.	shiny; glossy	1
犹犹豫豫	yóu yóu yù yù	adj.	hesitant	3
有必要	yǒu bìyào	vo.	necessary	4
有病	yǒu bìng	vo.	be sick; have illness	11
有的是	yǒu de shì		quite a lot; plenty	14
有点儿	yǒudiǎnr	adv.	a little bit; somewhat	1
有关	yǒuguān	v.	have something to do with	15
有利	yǒulì	adj.	advantageous; beneficial	19
有利于	yǒulìyú		be beneficial	12
有损	yǒusǔn	v.	harm; damage	7
有限	yǒuxiàn	adj.	limited	15
有学问	yǒu xuéwen		knowledgeable	1

友好	yǒuhǎo	adj.	friendly	6
幼儿园	yòu'éryuán	n.	kindergarten	15
鱼贩	yúfàn	n.	fish seller	11
于是	yúshì	conj.	so; then; thus; as a result	17
与	yǔ	conj.	and (literary)	7
与其	yǔqí	conj.	rather than; better than	12
遇到	yù dào	vc.	encounter; meet	9
郁闷	yùmèn	adj.	gloomy, depressed; be gloomy, be depressed	5
育新小区	Yùxīn Xiǎoqū	n.	Yuxin Subdivision	10
冤	yuān	adj.	be wronged; be treated unfairly	20
冤枉	yuānwang	v.	accuse (sb) wrongly	2
圆	yuán	adj.	round	1
缘分	yuánfèn	n.	predestined affinity; fate	13
员工	yuángōng	n.	employee; staff member	7
原来	yuánlái	adv./adj.	(it) turns out	10
原谅	yuánliàng	v.	forgive; pardon	4
元首	yuánshǒu	n.	head of state	19
约定	yuēdìng	v.	promise	12
月饼	yuèbing	n.	moon cake	1
月亮	yuèliang	n.	the moon	1
月票	yuèpiào	n.	monthly pass (for public transportation)	7
晕车	yùn chē	vo.	carsick	10

Z

咋呼	zhāhu	v.	talk; argue (as used in this story)	20
咱	zán	pron.	we, us; I, me	1
咱家	zán jiā		my (as used in this story)	10
咱俩	zán liǎ		two of us	3
咱们	zánmen	pron.	we; us (including the listener)	1
暂时	zànshí	adv.	for the time being; for the moment	15
脏话	zānghuà	n.	obscene; dirty or foul language	20
脏口	zāng kǒu	vo.	have a foul mouth	20
早班	zǎo bān		(see note 2)	20
早晨	zǎochén	t.	morning	2
早市	zǎoshì	n.	morning marketplace	11
责任	zérèn	n.	responsibility	9
怎么了	zěnme le		What happened? What's the matter?	2

怎么卖	zěnme mài		How much?	8
怎么着	zěnmezhe	pron.	what happened	5
炸酱面	zhájiàngmiàn	n.	noodles in fried bean sauce	1
粘贴	zhāntiē	v.	paste	5
站名	zhànmíng	n.	name of the bus stop or railroad station	7
站住	zhàn zhù	vc.	stop; halt	20
长出息	zhǎng chūxi	vo.	become more capable	20
掌握	zhǎngwò	v.	grasp; master	6
丈夫	zhàngfu	n.	husband	16
招	zhāo	v.	attract	18
招	zhāo	v.	provoke	20
招待	zhāodài	v.	receive; welcome	19
招呼	zhāohu	v./n.	greet; greeting	6
招聘	zhāopìn	v.	hire; search (for a position)	15
找错	zhǎo cuò	vc.	look for (somebody or something) at a wrong place; arrive at a wrong place	3
找错门	zhǎo cuò mén		come to a wrong door	3
找钱	zhǎo qián	vo.	give the change	13
赵叔/ 　赵叔叔	Zhào shū/ Zhào shūshū	N.	Uncle Zhao	3
哲人	zhérén	n.	sage; man of widsom	17
折腾	zhēteng	v.	do sth. over and over again; turn from side to side	16
这会儿	zhè huìr		now; at the moment	8
这么回事儿	zhème huí shìr		it was like this	11
这么着	zhèmezhe	pron.	in that case	1
这哪儿跟哪儿	zhè nǎr gēn nǎr		(see note 10)	9
着急	zháojí	adj.	worried; anxious	2
着呢	zhene	part.	(following an adjective to indicate degree) very; quite; greatly	1
着装	zhuózhuāng	n.	dressing	19
真诚	zhēnchéng	adj.	sincere; earnest	5
真实	zhēnshí	adj.	true; real	17
真是的	zhēn shì de		you are too much (as used in this story)	14
珍惜	zhēnxī	v.	value; cherish	17
争分夺秒	zhēng fēn duó miǎo		seize every minute	12
争气	zhēng qì	vo.	don't let down	18

拯救	zhěngjiù	v.	save; rescue	15
正	zhèng	adv.	right in the middle of（an action or a state）	5
正常	zhèngcháng	adj.	normal	11
正好	zhènghǎo	adv.	coindentally	8
正经	zhèngjing	adj.	decent; respectable	18
正式	zhèngshì	adj.	formal; official	19
正统	zhèngtǒng	adj.	authentic	19
正要	zhèng yào		be just about to	16
正装	zhèngzhuāng	n.	formal suit	19
证据	zhèngjù	n.	evidence; proof	8
证人	zhèng·rén	n.	witness	9
挣	zhèng	v.	earn	2
之	zhī	part.	（archaic and literary form for 的 indicating a possessive relationship）	5
知错就改	zhī cuò jiù gǎi		correct a mistake as soon as one realizes it	4
吱声	zī shēng	vo.	speak（colloq.）	13
知识	zhīshi	n.	knowledge; know how	15
直接	zhíjiē	adj.	direct	6
值	zhí	v.	be worth	13
值钱	zhíqián	adj.	valuable	9
纸	zhǐ	n.	paper	9
纸条	zhǐtiáo	n.	paper strip; scrip	14
指不定	zhǐbudìng	adv.	perhaps; maybe	4
指着	zhǐzhe	v.	（see note 9）	19
至于	zhìyú	v.	there is no need; not necessary	2
中标	zhòng biāo	vo.	get（or win）the bid	14
中国通	Zhōngguó tōng	n.	old China hand	1
中考	zhōngkǎo	n.	high school entrance examination	12
中年	zhōngnián	n.	middle age; middle aged	11
终于	zhōngyú	adv.	at last; in the end; finally	16
重新	chóngxīn	adv.	once again; once more	20
重要性	zhòngyàoxìng	n.	importance; significance	15
周到	zhōudào	adj.	thoughtful; considerate	16
猪八戒	Zhū Bājiè	N.	（see note 11）	18
猪肉	zhūròu	n.	pork	8
主人公	zhǔréngōng	n.	leading character（in a novel, a play, etc.）	17
注（点儿）意	zhù（diǎnr）yì	v.	be careful; pay attention	13

抓紧（点儿）	zhuā jǐn (diǎnr)		make good use of the time	13
时间	shíjiān			
专门	zhuānmén	adv.	especially (for a certain purpose)	16
转嫁	zhuǎnjià	v.	pass（the responsibility，blame，etc.）	16
			to someone else	
转	zhuàn	v.	stroll around	12
装饰品	zhuāngshìpǐn	n.	ornament; decoration	19
撞	zhuàng	v.	bump against (see note 9)	14
追不上	zhuī bu shàng	vc.	cannot catch up (with someone)	10
追上	zhuī shang	vc.	catch up (with sb.)	14
准	zhǔn	adj.	accurate; exact	18
仔细	zǐxì	adj.	careful; cautious	8
资料	zīliào	n.	data; information	7
资源	zīyuán	n.	resources	
自个儿	zìgěr	pron.	oneself; by oneself	18
字幕	zìmù	n.	caption; subtitle	17
自然	zìrán	adv./adj.	normally; certainly	10
自私	zìsī	adj.	selfish; self-centered	3
综合	zōnghé	v.	comprehensive	7
总	zǒng	adv.	always	4
总是	zǒngshì	adv.	always	17
走好	zǒu hǎo	vc.	bye (literally：walk carefully)	13
走人	zǒu rén	vo.	leave	8
祖先	zǔxiān	n.	ancestry; ancestors	12
尊敬	zūnjìng	v.	respect; honor	15
尊重	zūnzhòng	v.	respect	15
琢磨	zuómo	v.	ponder; figure out a way	13
琢磨	zuómo	v.	ponder; think over	2
做法	zuò·fǎ	n.	way of doing or making something	1
坐过了站	zuò guò le zhàn		(of a bus rider) miss the stop	7
坐好	zuò hǎo	vc.	get seated properly	1
做回主	zuò huí zhǔ	vo.	make the decision for (somebody)	1
做买卖	zuò mǎimai	vo.	do business	13
做人	zuò rén	vo.	conduct oneself	2
做生意	zuò shēngyi	vo.	do business	8
做小买卖	zuò xiǎo mǎimai	vo.	do small business; do little trading	8
作者	zuòzhě	n.	writer; author	5
作证	zuò zhèng	vo.	testify; serve as witness	9

附录二：注释索引 Notes Index

WINDOW TO CHINA